Beethoven's Orchestral Music

Unlocking the Masters Series, No. 33

Series Editor: Robert Levine

Unlocking the Masters

The highly acclaimed Unlocking the Masters series brings readers into the world of the greatest composers and their music. All books come with audio tracks taken from the world's foremost libraries of recorded classics, bringing the music to life.

> "With infectious enthusiasm and keen insight, the Unlocking the Masters series succeeds in opening our eyes, ears, hearts, and minds to the greatest composers"—Strings

Series Editor: Robert Levine

Ravel: A Listener's Guide, by Victor Lederer, 2000

Richard Strauss: An Owner's Manual, by David Hurwitz, 2000

Verdi: The Operas and Choral Works, by Victor Lederer, 2000

The Mahler Symphonies: An Owner's Manual, by David Hurwitz, 2004

Decoding Wagner: An Invitation to His World of Music Drama, by Thomas May, 2004

Exploring Haydn: A Listener's Guide to Music's Boldest Innovator, by David Hurwitz, 2005

Dvorak: Romantic Music's Most Versatile Genius, by David Hurwitz, 2005

Getting the Most Out of Mozart: The Instrumental Works, by David Hurwitz, 2005

Getting the Most Out of Mozart: The Vocal Works, by David Hurwitz, 2005

The Great Instrumental Works, by M. Owen Lee, 2006

Opera's First Master: The Musical Dramas of Claudio Monteverdi, by Mark Ringer, 2006

Shostakovich Symphonies and Concertos: An Owner's Manual, by David Hurwitz, 2006

Chopin: A Listener's Guide to the Master of the Piano, by Victor Lederer, 2006

Sibelius Orchestral Works: An Owner's Manual, by David Hurwitz, 2007

Beethoven's Symphonies: A Guided Tour, by John Bell Young, 2008

Puccini: A Listener's Guide, by John Bell Young, 2009

Schubert's Theater of Song: A Listener's Guide, by Mark Ringer, 2009

Liszt: A Listener's Guide, by John Bell Young, 2009

Schubert: A Survey of His Symphonic, Piano and Chamber Music, by John Bell Young, 2009
Bach's Choral Music: A Listener's Guide, by Gordon Jones, 2009
Bach's Keyboard Music: A Listener's Guide, by Victor Lederer, 2010
Beethoven's Piano Music: A Listener's Guide, by Victor Lederer, 2011
Bernstein's Orchestral Music: An Owner's Manual, by David Hurwitz, 2011
Beethoven's Chamber Music: A Listener's Guide, by Victor Lederer, 2012
Richard Strauss: An Owner's Manual, by David Hurwitz, 2014
Verdi: The Operas and Choral Works, by Victor Lederer, 2014
Ravel: A Listener's Guide, by Victor Lederer, 2015
C.P.E.: A Listener's Guide to the Other Bach, by David Hurwitz, 2016
Schumann: A Listener's Guide, by Victor Lederer, 2017
Listening to Handel: An Owner's Manual, by David Hurwitz, 2019
Listening to Mendelssohn: An Owner's Manual, by David Hurwitz, 2020
Bach's Operas of the Soul: A Listener's Guide to the Sacred Cantatas, by Mark Ringer, 2021
Beethoven's Orchestral Music: An Owner's Manual, by David Hurwitz, 2021
Berlioz: A Listener's Guide, by Victor Lederer, 2021

Beethoven's Orchestral Music
An Owner's Manual

David Hurwitz

AMADEUS PRESS

Lanham • Boulder • New York • London

Published by Amadeus Press
An imprint of The Rowman & Littlefield Publishing Group, Inc.
4501 Forbes Boulevard, Suite 200, Lanham, Maryland 20706
www.rowman.com

6 Tinworth Street, London SE11 5AL, United Kingdom

Copyright © 2021 by The Rowman & Littlefield Publishing Group, Inc.

All rights reserved. No part of this book may be reproduced in any form or by any electronic or mechanical means, including information storage and retrieval systems, without written permission from the publisher, except by a reviewer who may quote passages in a review.

Book design and composition by Snow Creative

Library of Congress Cataloging-in-Publication Data

ISBN 978-1-5381-3560-0 (pbk.)
ISBN 978-1-5381-3561-7 (electronic)

To Ali Javed,
the wizard of automotive Bluetooth

Contents

Acknowledgments	xi
Chronological Work List	xiii
Preface	xvii

Part 1: Listening to Beethoven — 1

Chapter 1: Beethoven and the Orchestra	3
Chapter 2: Beethoven's Dynamic Forms	21

Part 2: Overtures — 45

Discography	45
Chapter 3: Theatrical Overtures	49
Chapter 4: Concert Overtures	57
Interlude 1: Dance Music	67

Part 3: Concertos — 73

Discography	73
Chapter 5: General Introduction to Concerto Forms	81
Chapter 6: Piano Concertos	89
Chapter 7: Concerto and Romances for Violin	103

Chapter 8: Triple Concerto and Choral Fantasy	111
Interlude 2: Incidental Music	121

Part 4: Symphonies — 125

Discography	125
Chapter 9: Symphonies Nos. 1 and 2	133
Chapter 10: Symphonies Nos. 3 (*Eroica*) and 4	141
Chapter 11: Symphonies Nos. 5 and 6 (*Pastoral*)	159
Chapter 12: Symphonies Nos. 7 and 8	171
Chapter 13: *Wellington's Victory* (aka *Battle Symphony*)	183
Chapter 14: Symphony No. 9 (*Choral*)	189
Conclusion: The Quasi-Orchestral Beethoven	201
Track Listing	205

Acknowledgments

I want to thank very sincerely some of the people who helped to bring this project to completion. First, my editor, Bob Levine, whose comments and advice are invaluable. Also, thank you to the folks at Amadeus Press who have made working on this series such a pleasure, and the many friends who spent so much time with me talking about and listening to Beethoven, including Sören, Christophe, Styra, Silvia, Barry, Victor, Kenny, and Shawn—thank you, one and all!

Chronological Work List

The following list contains all of Beethoven's orchestral output worth mentioning. Missing are a few tiny interludes and such from the stage works that haven't been listed separately; but aside from those, the most significant omission is the Rondo in B-flat Major, WoO 6, for piano and orchestra, which originally served as the finale to the Second Piano Concerto (really the first in order of composition). This was completed and published by Carl Czerny, so there's some question as to how much of it is pure Beethoven. If you're curious, you can find it pretty easily in tandem with recordings of the piano concertos. There are also numerous fragments, some completed by others, which we don't need to bother with. Otherwise everything else is here, listed chronologically. As is often the case in this period, opus numbers generally reflect dates of publication rather than composition, which explains the sometimes paradoxical order of the earliest pieces.

1790

Musik zu einem Ritterballett (*Music for a Knight's Ballet*), WoO 1

1791

Twelve Contredanses, WoO 14

1795

Piano Concerto no. 1 in C Major, op. 15
Piano Concerto no. 2 in B-flat Major, op. 19
Twelve Minuets, WoO 7
Twelve German Dances, WoO 8

1798

Romance for Violin and Orchestra no. 2 in F Major, op. 50

1800

- Septet in E-flat Major, op. 20
- Symphony no. 1 in C Major, op. 21
- Piano Concerto no. 3 in C Minor, op. 37

1801

- *The Creatures of Prometheus*, overture and ballet music, op. 43

1802

- Symphony no. 2 in D Major, op. 36
- Romance for Violin and Orchestra no. 1 in G Major, op. 40

1804

- Triple Concerto for violin, cello, and piano in C Major, op. 56

1805

- Symphony no. 3 in E-flat Major (*Eroica*), op. 55
- *Leonore* Overture no. 2, op. 72a

1806

- *Leonore* Overture no. 3, op. 72b
- Piano Concerto no. 4 in G Major, op. 58
- Symphony no. 4 in B-flat Major, op. 60
- Violin Concerto in D Major, op. 61
- Piano Concerto in D Major, op. 61a

1807

- Piano Concerto in D Major, op. 61a (arrangement of the violin concerto)
- *Coriolan* Overture, op. 62
- *Leonore* Overture no. 1, op. 138

1808

- Symphony no. 5 in C Minor, op. 67
- Symphony no. 6 in F Major (*Pastoral*), op. 68
- Choral Fantasy, op. 80

1809

Piano Concerto no. 5 in E-flat Major (*Emperor*), op. 73

1810

Egmont, overture and incidental music, op. 84
String Quartet no. 11 in F Minor (*Serioso*), op. 95

1811

Die Ruinen von Athen (*The Ruins of Athens*), overture and incidental music, op. 113
König Stephan (*King Stephen*), overture and incidental music, op. 117

1812

Symphony no. 7 in A Major, op. 92
Symphony no. 8 in F Major, op. 93

1813

Wellington's Victory (*Battle Symphony*), op. 91
Triumphal March for *Tarpeja*, WoO 2a
Introduction to Act 2 of *Leonore*, WoO 2b

1814

Fidelio Overture, op. 72

1815

Zur Namensfeier (Name-Day Celebrations) Overture, op. 115
Funeral March for *Leonore Prohaska*, WoO 96

1818

Piano Sonata no. 29 in B-flat Major (*Hammerklavier*), op. 106

1822

Gratulations-Menuett, WoO 3
Die Weihe des Hauses (*The Consecration of the House*) Overture, op. 124

1824

- Symphony no. 9 in D Minor (*Choral*), op. 125

1825–1826

- Late String Quartets, op. 127, 130–32, 135
- Große Fuge, op. 133

Preface

Beethoven is manageable. According to the Beethoven-Haus in his birthplace of Bonn, Germany, he composed 722 pieces apportioned in three major categories: 138 works or groups of works with opus numbers (op.), 228 works or groups of works without an opus number (WoO), and 27 unfinished fragments. Although it may seem like a lot, it really isn't, because the music falls neatly into well-defined genres, none of which is intimidatingly large. For example, if you take the nine symphonies, seven concertos, and eleven overtures, you have all of the essential orchestral works. This survey reaches a couple of steps beyond the basics, encompassing about forty pieces in all, but nothing as intimidating and potentially time-consuming as Haydn's 107 symphonies, or Mozart's 41 to 60-something (depending on how you count), or Vivaldi's 600+ concertos and Bach's 200+ church cantatas. As I said, it's manageable.

More important, Beethoven is consistently great while being equally consistently original. Over the course of his life he abandoned the convention of gathering groups of works into a single opus (such as the six String Quartets, op. 18), and instead created a series of individual, unique masterpieces. This process is especially evident in the music for orchestra. Not a single major composition shares an opus number with any other, encouraging listeners to consider each on its own merits. Beethoven's reputation thus takes advantage of the idea that scarcity has value.

In other words, every big orchestral work that he wrote matters, perhaps not equally, but still significantly. We could lose, say, Mozart's Piano Concerto no. 19 or Haydn's Symphony no. 57 and, however regrettable, we wouldn't really be musically poorer, nor would our understanding of the composer's art suffer noticeably. But Beethoven without the *Pastoral* Symphony, the *Emperor* Concerto, or even the

Egmont Overture? Inconceivable. None of his large orchestral works is expendable. Each tells us something new and represents a marker on a clear evolutionary path, especially if we take into consideration the fact that they are spread relatively evenly over his entire career. Granted, other composers developed over a similarly wide range—Haydn comes to mind most obviously—but none packed so much audible progress into so few individual pieces. That makes Beethoven's personal artistic journey a distinctive and thrilling musical characteristic all by itself, never mind his music's manifold additional qualities.

Taking this particular aspect into consideration in the discussion that follows will, I hope, constitute one of two factors that distinguish this book from the countless others about Beethoven and his music. I will not spend time on unnecessary biographical trivia. Beethoven's life was pretty miserable. He went deaf. He was irascible, paranoid, and often obnoxious. His personal hygiene in later years was disgusting. Nevertheless, and this is a point forgotten all too frequently—the vast majority of his music is joyous, indeed giddy. Yes, he could plumb the depths of tragedy as had few before him, but the works that do that are exceptions. Too much emphasis on dark but often titillating biographical detail threatens to conceal this crucial musical reality.

I also will not talk much about Beethoven's non-orchestral pieces, or his vocal works with orchestra (with two obvious exceptions). These are fascinating subjects for another day. Instead, I will stick to the "less is more" theory that served Beethoven himself so well and ask that you approach each orchestral piece individually, as a unique musical statement that speaks to us with immediacy and relevance. This does not mean that the music will be presented devoid of any useful context, but rather that the context will be explicitly musical and relate clearly to the experience of listening to the work at hand.

The second factor separating this book from the pack will be the extensive listing and discussion of recordings of all of the music covered.[1] I can't stress enough how important is this aspect, and how much

---

1. For simplicity's sake, I identify recordings by participating orchestra and conductor. Additional information is provided where necessary. Unfortunately, naming record labels is no longer especially helpful due to mergers, licensing deals, and the availability of digital media and streaming services. As a rule of thumb, and especially

more rewarding will be your encounter with Beethoven if you take it seriously. All great music is basically self-explanatory. Recent studies in the psychology of music have shown that reading a description of a piece before listening to it for the first time may make that initial encounter less pleasurable than a situation where you are listening "cold" but with an open mind.

It seems that knowing in advance what you are supposed to hear limits the active use of your imagination, restricts your subjective experience of the music's many expressive possibilities, causes anxiety about your ability to identify the specific elements previously mentioned, and may even lead to frustration if you don't notice them or agree with their prior characterization. Think of it this way: it's far more rewarding to listen to an unfamiliar piece, read about it, and then be able to say, "Aha! I heard that, too," than it would be to read one person's description of it before listening and come away annoyed from the encounter thinking, "What the hell was he talking about?" Either way it's the same piece of music, but how you approach it really does matter.

On the other hand, reading about a piece of music after you have heard it can deepen your appreciation, offer new insights, or suggest avenues to understanding and enjoyment that might not have struck you at first acquaintance; but to realize these benefits to the fullest extent, you have to know what the topic of the conversation is going into it. That means either attending concerts regularly—an expensive, haphazard, and time-consuming process—or listening to conveniently available recordings. Beethoven being as popular as he is, I assume that you probably have heard some of this music and already have a pretty strong desire to hear more, but familiar or not, that doesn't change my point: if you're going to invest the time, you should set yourself up to

---

with respect to older recordings by "big-name" artists, try to stick to the historical "major labels" and their attendant sub-labels. These are (or were) RCA, Columbia (now Sony Classical), Deutsche Grammophon, Philips (now Decca), and EMI (now Warner Classics). Avoid obvious pirates or alleged "historical" reissues of live performances. These are mostly aimed at connoisseurs who know exactly what they are getting. Performers appearing on smaller, independent labels are often easier to source because they haven't been repeatedly exploited or reissued over the decades, but no hard-and-fast rules apply. It's an adventure.

get the most out of it and have the most enjoyable experience possible. So it's music first, book second.

Beethoven is one of the most frequently recorded of all composers, with dozens, even hundreds of versions of many of his most famous pieces released by just about every classical artist, major or minor. Digital media have made the music cheaper and more freely accessible than ever. There are performances for every taste, by great orchestras, great conductors dead or alive, musicians specializing in historical performance practices, and local schools of playing and interpretation. Although the listings are necessarily personal, I have tried to include interpretations generally acknowledged in the critical fraternity to be "reference" versions, and I took suggestions from many friends, both musicians and avid collectors. In other words, I tried to make the selection as inclusive as possible, one that will, at one point or another, offer you a tangible way to hear the music from multiple perspectives.

For this reason, the lists of recommended recordings always precede discussion of the works in question, but they are not in any way intended to be limiting. That would be neither wise nor possible, especially when you consider that the history of Beethoven's music on recordings is basically the history of recordings more generally. If you have your own collection, or your own preferences, or simply can't find a particular listed title, feel free to take matters into your own hands. There is no right way or wrong way, as long as you're listening to the music in some fashion.

Keeping these observations in mind, you can use this book several ways. Dip in at will, listen to something, and then read about it; or you might prefer a more systematic program. The book is organized like a typical concert writ large, moving from small pieces to larger: overtures, concertos, and then symphonies. In between, a couple of "interludes" deal with Beethoven's dance music and his pieces written as accompaniment to the spoken theater. You also might adopt a chronological approach, for which I have provided a list of all of the music discussed organized by date of composition. A couple of introductory chapters on general topics—Beethoven and the orchestra, plus his handling of musical form—will get you started.

Finally, let me close with an observation and a confession. The observation is this: Beethoven is so famous, such an integral part of our musical culture—even popular culture—that approaching his music can be intimidating. I am a great believer in the audience's rights. As long as you put in the time to listen with intention, then your feelings—positive or negative—are as valid as anyone's. That leads me to a confession as an example of what I mean. I've never much cared for the *Eroica* Symphony, by common consent one of Beethoven's very greatest works. I've heard it countless times, own dozens of recordings, and believe I understand it pretty well. A great performance of it thrills me. But do I love it? No. It's an occasional indulgence, and that's just how it is. I'm fine with it. So, even though this is BEETHOVEN, listen fearlessly and critically. Beethoven wasn't perfect, nor is all of his music equally appealing to all listeners. He might have cursed you out for your opinion, but he would have been the first to grant your right to have one.

Part 1

Listening to Beethoven

Beethoven and the Orchestra

Beethoven essentially invented the modern orchestra. That may sound like an extravagant claim, but it's true to the historical facts. He didn't do it in Vienna, or in the German-speaking lands, or even necessarily by design. Believe it or not, it happened in Paris. On August 9, 1828, a little more than a year after his death, conductor and violinist François-Antoine Habeneck (1781–1849) led the inaugural concert of the Orchestre de la Société des Concerts du Conservatoire (the Orchestra of the Conservatory Concert Society). This ensemble, containing the finest musicians available—including numerous professors at the Paris Conservatory and other instrumental virtuosos active in the French capital—was formed specifically for the purpose of presenting all of Beethoven's major orchestral works to the French public. That first concert featured the *Eroica* Symphony. It was both a resounding success and a cultural milestone, immediately recognized as such.

If the Paris Conservatory was at that time the world's most prestigious, then the orchestra was its crown jewel. It became the model for virtually all of the great European orchestras that followed and set new standards for the few already in existence. Beethoven's music provided its calling card. In its first twenty years, the Société des Concerts gave 318 performances of his works, including 188 of the symphonies alone, all in "seasons" comprising (initially) only six individual programs. Of course, we need to bear in mind that in the days before recordings, a limited repertoire combined with more frequent repetition was essential. If you wanted to hear the most recent big hit or novelty, and the concert hall could barely seat one thousand patrons, and no significant competition or alternative was available, you had to hope that the same pieces would appear frequently in response to public demand—and so they did.

Prior to the French orchestra's establishment, and for a long time afterward, performance standards were, to put it mildly, variable, and regular seasons sporadic. Most ensembles were either the private property of wealthy aristocrats or else organized on an ad hoc basis for a single event or limited series. These invariably were scheduled during a time when the rich folk would be in their urban residences—usually before the annual summer outbreaks of cholera, plague, smallpox, or what have you. Musicians were expected to perform new, unfamiliar works after a single rehearsal, or even at sight. Haydn offers the iconic example of eighteenth-century orchestral culture. Most of his symphonies were composed for the very small, private orchestra of his employers, the noble Esterházy family. The later "Paris" and "London" Symphonies were commissioned for public concerts in those cities, and the size of the ensemble was correspondingly larger.

When Haydn received an honorary doctorate at Oxford, at which a couple of his latest symphonies were performed, he felt obliged to beg the organizers to hold at least one rehearsal in advance. Beethoven, in premiering his latest works at his own benefit concerts, had to hire and pay his own players, print and sell his own tickets, lease the venue, and in general make all of the necessary arrangements himself. The results sometimes were disastrous. A concert featuring orchestral music as the main item was a sometime thing, for both financial and logistical reasons. From the artistic point of view, instrumental pieces took a back seat to vocal music, both sacred and secular. Well into the nineteenth century, it was unusual to find a purportedly orchestral concert that did not feature a noted singer or two as an added attraction.

However, from 1828 onward, it became possible to arrange a program in which the featured symphony was the main event. Beethoven made this possible. His works put orchestral writing on an even footing with music in other genres. The symphonies and concertos are, for the most part, lengthier and more difficult than any that had come before. They require many rehearsals to master and sound their best, the kind of results only possible to obtain from a regularly constituted, full-time ensemble. Even more important, they reward the effort in terms of their brilliance, virtuosity, excitement, and expressivity. All orchestral music is public, in a sense, but Beethoven's is designed for the *general public*—literally, for everyone within range of hearing. Its lack of a sung text only enhances its universality, and in the one symphony where Beethoven does employ singers—the Ninth—the text is explicitly *about* universality: the brotherhood of all mankind.

Critics, even those who acknowledged Beethoven's genius, often found him loud, crude, and sometimes obscure, but audiences loved him. He became a bankable commodity. The Orchestre de la Société des Concerts du Conservatoire continued to feature Beethoven on its programs for the next 140 years, until it was disbanded by the French government and absorbed into the newly established Orchestre de Paris in the late 1960s. It was a sad loss: the only ensemble that could boast of having preserved a consistent, unbroken performance tradition dating back to Beethoven's own lifetime. Over the course of the virulently nationalistic nineteenth century, German ensembles assumed the mantle of Beethoven's true heirs; today, the "historically informed" performance movement makes similar claims, but none of them can boast of a similar pedigree.

Fortunately, the legacy of the Paris Conservatory Orchestra in Beethoven was captured just in time, in the late 1950s, when French EMI recorded a complete symphony cycle under the baton of the excellent, very underrated German conductor Carl Schuricht. These fine performances, recorded mostly in very good mono sound (the Ninth can be heard in its first stereo release on the Testament label), have seldom left the catalog, and for good reason. The orchestra's consistent rhythmic freshness, textural transparency, lean and wiry strings, characterful woodwinds, and piercing brass seem made for Beethoven, and the players willingly embrace Schuricht's consistently lively and exuberant interpretations. Later cycles certainly feature better sonics, more polished ensembles, and perhaps more probing conducting, but none more idiomatic or committed than this.

According to contemporary reports, the Orchestre de la Société des Concerts du Conservatoire at its inaugural concerts numbered about eighty-six players, and thereafter settled down to a regular roster of eighty—roughly the size of a modern orchestra today. Don't let anyone tell you that because Beethoven often had to make do with many fewer musicians, he planned his orchestral works for these smaller forces, and they sound better when presented that way. The numerous chamber orchestras and period instrument ensembles active today operate under the same financial constraints that Beethoven did. To be sure, the music can be presented with reduced personnel, and a great performance speaks for itself (we will mention a few), but mini-Beethoven is seldom preferable to the full-size version and certainly enjoys no special sanction or claim to authenticity.

Early music groups, in particular, often make a fetish of stripping every piece they touch to the bare minimum number of performers required. To this pernicious habit I can only quote the great English writer on music Donald Francis Tovey, who memorably claimed, "Scholarship itself is not obliged to insist on the restoration of conditions that ought never to have existed." No problem of balance or texture in Beethoven cannot be solved with a full-size ensemble, and large forces always can be reduced for especially intimate passages; but if you start small, you're stuck with it. You can't cheat physics. Beethoven's music is big—in scope, in vision, in expression, and in sheer sonic splendor. A performance that doesn't deliver these qualities, never mind the number of participants, invariably misses the point.

One sure sign of the general perception of Beethoven's "bigness" has been the historical tendency to recast some of his chamber works in orchestral garb, especially the late string quartets, the *Hammerklavier* Piano Sonata, and the early Septet, op. 20. For this reason, I include them in the work listing at the front of this book and will offer a brief discussion of this "quasi-orchestral" Beethoven on disc by way of conclusion in the last chapter. The idea that Beethoven's music, in its energy and scope, bursts the bounds of smaller forces has always been with us, and it says a lot about his natural affinity for the symphony orchestra that it has been taken so seriously (and, in many cases, implemented so successfully).

Accordingly, whereas Beethoven's ensemble writing often sounds strikingly different from that of his predecessors, the results he gets arise not so much from the multiplicity and variety of instruments involved as from how he uses them and from the range and breadth of his musical ideas. It is true that he enlarged the symphonic orchestra by adding piccolo, contrabassoon, and trombones, although he was not the first to do so—just the best. All of these instruments appear in the Fifth and Ninth Symphonies, and the latter features additional percussion (cymbals, bass drum, and triangle) besides. On the other hand, Haydn had used an ensemble of similar size two decades earlier in his last grand oratorio, *The Seasons*, of 1801. In fact, Haydn does his star pupil one instrument better by adding a third trumpet in the closing chorus.

What Beethoven did, however, was take these hitherto exotic extras, familiar visitors to operatic and theatrical orchestras, and use them in a purely instrumental setting, apart from any pictorial or incidental associations that they might have had. For example, trombones often were found accompanying the choir in liturgical music, or backing supernatural events such as Don Giovanni's descent into hell in the last act of Mozart's famous opera. When they turn up, with the piccolo and contrabassoon, in the celebratory finale of Beethoven's Fifth Symphony, their presence contributes to music simultaneously higher, lower, louder, and more explosive than anything ever heard before.

Beethoven's regular demand for trumpets and timpani was also extraordinary for its time. Although routinely called for in music of a festive or military character, their presence in the symphony orchestra was by no means a fact to be taken for granted. Trumpeters and drummers usually were members of the local town guard or military garrison, not full-time players of "art music." Haydn established them as permanent participants in the ensemble with his twelve "London" Symphonies. Beethoven ratified this decision, and in effect made it standard. All of his major orchestral works require trumpets and drums, with the single exception of the Second Piano Concerto (actually his first in order of writing). From Beethoven on, it was not the presence of these instruments in the orchestra that was unusual but, rather, their absence.

Far more significant than these innovations, however, was the manner in which Beethoven treated the individual instrumental sections. The classical orchestra basically consisted of a large body of strings opposed to a smaller assortment of woodwinds (flutes, oboes, bassoons, and eventually clarinets), a couple of horns, and finally trumpets and timpani to mark the rhythm and add pizzazz to loud passages. Haydn and

Mozart already understood that the key to great orchestration lay in the handling of the woodwinds, both as solos and in groups. The reason for this is simple: the winds (including horns for our purposes) have the most coloristic variety within their section and therefore offer the best opportunity both to characterize a melodic line and prevent monotony in otherwise simple accompaniments. Beethoven took this process a step further, emancipating the wind section and using it with unprecedented freedom and imagination.

You can hear this from the very first notes of the First Symphony, a bright pair of chords for the woodwinds backed by pizzicato (plucked) strings. It's a new sound, but even more important, the timbre draws attention to the amusing fact that these chords harmonically represent not a beginning but an ending. As if realizing their error, the woodwinds try again with another pair of similarly misplaced chords. Only at the third attempt does the rest of the orchestra enter with confirmation that they've finally gotten things right. It is absolute acceptance of this odd start. From this humorous example we can conclude that Beethoven's exploration of new colors and timbres was not gratuitous but, rather, a significant enhancement of the music's expressive meaning. It is, in short, an integral aspect of his personal musical language and to what later became the symphonic ideal: it should include no effects without causes, and all of the various parts should work together in furtherance of the music's ultimate goal.

To this end, Beethoven gave difficult and surprising solos, both singly and in sections, to members of the orchestra unaccustomed to the spotlight. The Violin Concerto begins with its main motive gently tapped out by the timpani, of all things. He also adopted unconventional tunings to permit the drums an extra degree of participatory freedom. The solos in the Ninth's second movement are justly famous. Less frequently mentioned but no less remarkable are the soft, two-note timpani chords in the closing bars of the same work's Adagio. The middle section of the Third (*Eroica*) Symphony's Scherzo is a trio for three horns, another instrument that assumed new importance under his watch. Beethoven rightly can be said to have discovered the power and poetry of the double basses, whether in their thunderstorm rumblings in the Sixth (*Pastoral*) Symphony, or their "speaking" recitative at the start of the Ninth's finale. In every one of these and many other instances, which we will discuss in their appropriate places, the unusual colors serve a genuine musical purpose in addition to being inherently ear catching.

Beethoven's orchestral writing has many proprietary characteristics more generally that he either invented outright or appropriated and used in an individual way. The more you listen, the more obvious these musical "figures of speech" become. Some of them were absorbed into the common practice of Romantic music, used by later composers so frequently that we easily forget their original source and no longer associate them with Beethoven specifically.

Perhaps the best known of these is the big concluding windup. You know what I mean: a series of loud, crashing chords for the full orchestra, separated by suspenseful pauses, often accompanied by a loud roll on the drums. Just about everyone who came later used this ending, especially to conclude triumphant finales. Brahms, Tchaikovsky, and Dvořák hardly could have functioned without it. These memorable concluding bars are, however, in Beethoven at least, the outcome of a larger formal process, one that we might conveniently call

The Coda That Just Won't Quit

A musical "coda" (Italian for "tail") is exactly what the word implies: an added bit at the end designed to bring a piece to a satisfactory close. In its simplest form, it consists of a "cadence," or harmonic formula, that permits the music to conclude in its home key. Most codas in the classical period are relatively short—or they were until Haydn got his hands on them and realized he could expand the coda into an independent section containing a good bit of extra thematic development and dramatic incident. Indeed, the length of the coda doesn't really matter as long as it gives the feeling of arriving at a firm conclusion. The reasons for this we'll talk about in more detail in the next chapter. For now, all we need to know is that Beethoven took Haydn's initial concept and ran with it.

The iconic example of "the coda that just won't quit" occurs in the finale of the Fifth Symphony. Its triumphant musical procession, which already has been chugging along for a good six or seven minutes, shows no sign of stopping until suddenly it pulls up short with a series of abrupt, final-sounding chords, interrupted by the bassoons playing what seems like an entirely new theme. It's not, but for reasons you might find it hard to put your finger on, when that seemingly new tune appears, you just *know* that the music is starting to look for the right ending. All of the ensuing pauses and digressions, the abrupt dynamic contrasts from very loud to very soft, the climaxes that rise and fall, are Beethoven's way of stopping the musical juggernaut that his finale has unleashed.

However, because the movement has accumulated so much physical energy, this process takes time—about two and a half minutes to be exact—with the added bonus that the coda doesn't merely stop the music dead but ratifies or even enhances its expressive point: a feeling of boundless, unquenchable joy in victory. The result, then, isn't just one of the many usual concluding formulas but, rather, an active search for exactly the *right* ending, both to the finale specifically and the entire, half-hour-long symphony in general. When it finally arrives, the last gesture couldn't be more emphatic; and if you're tempted to chuckle along the way, then that's part of Beethoven's plan, too. It's entirely characteristic of him: a work that begins in frenzied fury ends in equally frenzied high spirits.

Perhaps the most extreme, and funniest, case of the coda that just won't quit in all of Beethoven occurs in the finale of the Eighth Symphony. That movement, which plays for about seven to eight minutes, contains 502 bars (or "measures") of music, with the coda starting at measure 267. In other words, it occupies about half of the movement.

However, not all codas are loud and boisterous, even in otherwise quick pieces. The coda to the finale of the *Pastoral* Symphony is peaceful and nostalgic. The Funeral March second movement in the *Eroica* has an extraordinary coda that's mostly very hushed and about as sorrowful as music gets. That in the Adagio of the Ninth, on the other hand, is radiant. Some codas begin imperceptibly, whereas others (in the finale of the *Eroica*, the *Egmont* Overture, or the *Leonore* Overtures nos. 2 and 3) are fully independent, almost detachable episodes. All of them give Beethoven the opportunity to expand the music's expressive range and find new meaning in its basic material. None are formulaic.

Along the way to one of Beethoven's proprietary endings, especially in quick music, chances are good that we'll encounter another of his characteristic orchestral fingerprints:

The Beethoven Crescendo

One of the marks of a great composer is his ability to personalize even the most mundane musical gesture. The crescendo—that is, the dynamic nuance of gradually getting louder—is as old as music itself, but only in the classical period did composers begin to notate the practice precisely and regularly, as opposed to leaving it to the discretion of the performers. Its desirability as an orchestral effect is obvious, and it became a mid-eighteenth-century specialty of the virtuoso ensemble in residence at the court of Mannheim, Germany. Visitors flocked to hear the Mannheim orchestra in order to experience the famous crescendo, and a talented group of resident composers, headed by the Stamitz family, happily provided new works to meet the demand.

Beethoven's habit of marking his scores in great detail, combined with his uniquely energetic, dramatic approach to composition generally, made him a "natural" when it came to the strategic employment of the crescendo. He was also lucky historically. Orchestral effects such as those featured in Mannheim had not yet become routine, so Beethoven had a relatively open field when it came to devising proprietary methods. Crescendos can be made in countless ways. You can simply play a tune, gradually increasing the volume. You can swell individual notes, chords, or groups of chords. The crescendo can be short, long, and everything in between. Most such options are generic and, therefore, impossible to stamp with any degree of individuality.

The crescendos we want to consider, however, are more specialized. They are distinctive, extended passages whose main purpose is to build tension by getting steadily louder, introducing at their peak an important theme or gesture by way of a climax. Beethoven's Italian contemporary Gioachino Rossini, for example, wrote opera overtures that became famous for the "Rossini crescendo," a brief tune repeated over and over, gaining volume and intensity, and exploding in a "tutti" (full orchestral) passage of great brilliance and verve. The "Rossini crescendo" was more than a simple expressive nuance added to an important harmony or melody; it was a definite musical object all by itself, one displaying a clear formal function. This is what made it special.

Beethoven's personal take on the crescendo is similar to Rossini's, in that it consists of a distinct episode that relies on the accumulated weight of repetition as the various instruments enter and the volume increases. Unlike Rossini, however, Beethoven does not employ a new "crescendo tune," repeating it with little variation. Instead, he takes a brief group of notes—a motive—clearly derived from the main thematic material and builds his crescendo either through obsessive repetition, or, even more arrestingly, through reiterations of tiny, rhythmically identical variants. Typically, the strings play the motive while the winds support them with sustained chords. This may sound technical, but the result comes across as spontaneous, attention grabbing, and extremely effective in practice. As the music gets louder, and the motive rapidly spreads through the full orchestra, the crescendo seems to come at you from all sides, generating an extra degree of nervous intensity and forward momentum.

If the job of the coda is to steer the symphonic drama safely home, the crescendos are musical locomotives. They execute transitions from one theme to another, develop previously heard ideas in a dynamically charged way, and propel the music over major sectional breaks. As part of a movement's connective tissue, they belong in the category of what I call "motion music." This idea will be more clearly defined and discussed in the next chapter. For now, all you need to know is that Beethoven's proprietary crescendos generally occur around and between the important tunes.

For example, all three overtures: *Egmont* and *Leonore* 2 and 3, previously noted for their distinctive codas, present their initial allegro themes twice, first softly, then loudly. In order to get from one statement to the other, Beethoven features a substantial passage of crescendo texture based on a bit of the principal idea. In the first movements of the Fifth and Seventh Symphonies, as well as the Fourth Piano Concerto, distinctive crescendos assist with the transitions between the first and second themes (later we'll call them "subjects," but "themes" will do for now). In the *Emperor* Concerto, a typical crescendo introduces the return of the work's virtuosic opening measures about two-thirds of the way through the first movement. An especially explosive example occurs in the same spot in the Eighth Symphony.

Beethoven's most systematic use of the crescendo, however, occurs in the first movement of the *Pastoral* Symphony. Here, we do find one in an expected place: between the two contrasting statements—first soft, then loud—of the initial tune, but the second theme is virtually nothing *but* a crescendo backed by a simple bit of melody, while two gigantic ones comprise most of the central "development" section. Indeed, we might legitimately say that the entire piece is organized around the concept of the crescendo, rising and falling in great waves of unusually mellow and euphonious sound (remember, it's supposed to be "pastoral"). The whole movement stands as a remarkable testament to Beethoven's imaginative use of simple ideas—the real nuts and bolts of music—to create strikingly original results. Nothing else in the symphonic literature is quite like it.

If the crescendo describes one of Beethoven's most important vehicles for achieving forward momentum—we might call it movement along the horizontal plane—we should also consider its companion technique as well, used to create a feeling of vertical movement. This doesn't have a technical term at all—not in Beethoven, and not in music generally—so we'll have to make up our own; yet it's one of the most telling of his stylistic fingerprints. We'll call it

The Beethoven Bounce

A "Beethoven Bounce" is simply a repeated jumping from low pitch to high, or high to low, that gives the impression of bouncing up and down (or down and up), usually vigorously, but sometimes more gently. It can occur anywhere, but it always has the effect of energizing the musical texture. The leaping start of the Ninth Symphony's Scherzo is one example, as is the jerky rhythmic figure at the opening of the Fourth Symphony's slow movement. Beethoven uses the bounce to imitate lightning bolts in the storm section of the *Pastoral* Symphony.

Because it's a purely rhythmic idea, usually made up of just a few repeated notes or chords, when it occurs at the end of a melodic section, the bounce often gives the impression that Beethoven has gotten so excited that organized thought (i.e., a tune) can no longer contain his enthusiasm, so the music instead resorts to a kind of primal, physical gesticulation. You can hear especially jolly examples at the start of the *Fidelio* Overture and at the close of the exposition sections of the Seventh Symphony's first movement (more on "expositions" in the next chapter) and the Fourth Symphony's finale. The *Coriolan* Overture begins with an angry bounce, and because the piece basically is one long temper tantrum, it features several others once it gets going. The initial entry of the soloist in the first movement of the Violin Concerto, on the other hand, offers an example of the bounce at its most graceful as the violin gently rises into view. Beethoven even finds room for a pair of bounces at the first two loud outbursts in the *Eroica* Symphony's funeral march.

Beethoven discovered the value of the bounce early in his career. It's one of the things that makes the outer movements of the First Symphony sound less like Haydn and Mozart and more like the new guy in town. The classical style that Beethoven inherited relied on certain harmonic and rhythmic formulas, especially to mark the ends of major sections. Remember "cadences" from our discussion of the coda? These tend to lower the music's energy level by inserting a pause or coming to a point of rest. Beethoven, on the other hand, likes to keep things moving as much as possible, and using the bounce at these points accomplishes this. The music may break off for a moment, but its energy and momentum carry over into the next passage or section.

Another advantage to being bouncy has to do with Beethoven's handling of rhythm more generally. He loves syncopation—the practice of accenting what ordinarily would sound as weaker beats. For example, if you're writing in three-quarter time (3/4 as notated musically, aka waltz tempo), you hear the basic rhythm as ONE-two-three, ONE-two-three, and so forth. Beethoven, in common with most other composers, uses this particular meter very often, including in the first movement of the *Eroica* Symphony and in the main body of the *Egmont* Overture, two of his most heroic-sounding and dramatic compositions. The reason he liked triple time (as it's often called) is the same reason we dance to it: it has an extra lift and sense of motion. However, an obvious waltz rhythm hardly would do such serious, indeed epic, music justice.

One of Beethoven's solutions, then, is to throw the accents onto the weaker beats, often joining together the second and third: one-TWO-THREE, one-TWOTHREE. This pattern produces a distinctive bounce. You can hear it in the first movement of the *Eroica* at the close of the exposition from measure 109 (if you follow scores). In this case, the bouncing rhythm accompanies a melody, as it does from measure 665 in the coda, right after the triumphant statement of the main theme on the trumpets. In the *Egmont* Overture, on the other hand, Beethoven reverses this pattern at measure 110: ONETWO-three, ONETWO-three, to close the exposition in a mood of high excitement. Dividing the three beats in a measure unequally and using syncopation, combined with appropriate scoring, generates the kind of forward impulse and, well, *bounce* that gives Beethoven's music so much of its distinctive power. You might not want to dance to it, exactly, but you feel the rhythm in your gut nonetheless.

You may find it curious that the three issues just discussed—codas, crescendos, and the Beethoven bounce—have absolutely nothing to do with the part of the music that most listeners probably care about above all others: the tunes. Indeed, none of them would matter so much if Beethoven did not write great tunes, too, but these are best discussed in their individual places. Moreover, the large orchestral works aren't just about presenting the melody; they are about what becomes of it over the course of a movement. This, in turn, depends on the musical environment that the tunes inhabit, one that contains a wide range of additional ideas and gestures specifically tailored to the orchestral medium.

What I have tried to do here is describe some of the more prominent and interesting features of that environment. It could be that if you took my initial advice and listened to some of the music before reading this, you already have noticed some or all of these elements. If so, you should feel confident in your superior listening prowess. If not, then you have some advance news of what to listen for, and hopefully this brief discussion will prove helpful. Either way, these various techniques and compositional strategies combine with the famous (and not so famous) tunes to produce Beethoven's music in large forms. In the next chapter, we will take a close look at those as well.

Before doing that, however, I want to mention a few points that relate to recordings of the orchestral works that you should keep in mind to avoid getting snookered when shopping.

The first of these concerns Beethoven's metronome markings. The self-proclaimed inventor of the metronome, Johann Mälzel (or Maelzel), was associated with Beethoven and got him to suggest mechanical tempo markings (in beats per minute) for the individual movements of the symphonies. These always have been controversial for a number of reasons, not the least being that Beethoven was quite deaf at the time he chose them, and it's very doubtful that he ever heard performances at the more questionable designated speeds.

It is also pretty clear that some of the quicker tempos would have been impossible for orchestras at the time, and that the metronome markings do not take into account the natural fluctuations of pulse that would have been taken for granted both then and now in any normally expressive performance. Beethoven himself had reservations on that account. Some of them, such as those in the coda of the Ninth Symphony's finale, seem to run counter to other tempo and expressive indications and seemingly contradict the plain character of the music. Nevertheless, the metronome markings can be helpful in indicating relative speeds between movements and in suggesting proportional tempo relationships.

Interestingly, a contemporary account of Beethoven's Ninth mentions a duration of sixty-five minutes in total, basically the same as an average performance today, give or take a few minutes either way. Aside from anecdotal evidence such as this, we have no way of knowing what the parameters for an "average" timing would have been in Beethoven's era. Doubtless they would have been much wider than they are now due to huge disparities in the quality of early nineteenth-century orchestras, plus the lack of homogeneity resulting from the absence of a generally acknowledged performing tradition—never mind the extensive documentation of that tradition that recordings afford modern players and conductors.

Today the situation obviously is quite different. Our superbly trained musicians often are able to play the music at Beethoven's theoretically recommended speeds, but that doesn't mean that they should. Sometimes the results can be exhilarating; at others, the music comes across as a garbled mess. Issues such as room acoustics, accent marks, and articulation signs all act as a break on the mindless application of a designated tempo. Where this becomes an issue is when conductors and their record producers try to use "authentic tempos" as a selling point. Don't buy it. Nothing, and I really mean *nothing*, suggests that the metronome numbers that have come down to us as Beethoven's markings are invariably correct, let alone binding on the players or in some way sacrosanct. Any statement to the contrary is mere puffery.

The same observations apply to claims by performers using new, "critical," or "Urtext" ("original text") editions of scores. With very few exceptions, these simply are a publisher's ploy to keep Beethoven's music in copyright. The differences between the latest version and the standard prints, in Beethoven anyway, usually are vanishingly few, often trivial, and likely to be inaudible in performance. For some composers and circumstances, the publication of such editions truly is a heroic scholarly undertaking—in Italian and French grand opera, for example—but Beethoven's orchestral scores are a known quantity, and the choice of one edition over another is neither a meaningful artistic decision nor a legitimate selling point.

Finally, we need to discuss the question of "authentic" or "period" instruments and the "historically informed performance" (HIP) movement as it applies to Beethoven. At its inception, in the 1960s and '70s, the main purpose of HIP was to permit us to hear reams of hitherto disregarded baroque and early music in circumstances as close as possible to what we believe audiences of the time experienced. This was tremendously exciting, indeed revelatory, and the scholarly apparatus that supported this effort has since evolved into an entirely new discipline: "applied musicology." However, as the HIP movement began encroaching on the standard classical and romantic repertoire, its achievements began to sound less and less impressive.

In the first place, the music of Haydn, Mozart, and especially Beethoven, never has been out of the active repertoire. Today's modern instruments, orchestras, and performance traditions were shaped by the need to play this very music in conditions as near to ideal as possible.

Also, as I mentioned at the start of this chapter, the best orchestras in Beethoven's day—indeed, the only ones we would recognize as fully professional ensembles featuring something approaching modern performance standards—were likely far closer to what we are accustomed to hearing now than they are to any HIP organization, especially the ones that specialize in baroque repertoire and only make the occasional foray into later music.

Indeed, our distance from Beethoven himself, historically speaking, has been grossly exaggerated. Great conductors born within fifty years of Beethoven's death lived to make magnificent recordings of his music, and some of them worked well into the era of stereo long-playing records. I'm thinking of men such as Arturo Toscanini (1867–1957), Pierre Monteux (1875–1964), or Bruno Walter (1876–1962). The first conductor to record a complete Beethoven symphony cycle, Felix Weingartner (d. 1942), was born in 1863, only thirty-six years after Beethoven's death. Even Carl Schuricht, whose Paris Beethoven cycle I just mentioned, was born in 1880. You can't convince me that some young HIP hotshot has a stronger connection to the musical aesthetics of the nineteenth century than they did and, consequently, knows how to play Beethoven more idiomatically. The audible evidence is ready to hand.

Many of the most effective "innovations" promulgated by the HIP movement, such as swifter tempos, certain approaches to phrasing and articulation, or the use of timpani with hard sticks and a willingness to play specific passages literally as regards instrumental balance and dynamics, have been completely co-opted by standard orchestras and their conductors, with results that tend to sound far superior than anything achievable on period instruments. After all, these orchestras still boast the finest players, the best-quality instruments, and a corporate identity and ensemble standard that no "pickup" group (which is what most HIP ensembles are) can hope to match. It's telling that one of the most respected and authoritative founding fathers of the historical performance movement, Nikolaus Harnoncourt, when he came to record his Beethoven cycle, used a modern string ensemble mixed with a few period winds for the sake of their unique timbres.

The applied musicology crowd simply gets some details wrong. This is a discussion for another time, but suffice it to say that its more fanatical proponents have an understandable tendency to give greater weight to anything that makes a performance sound different from today's norm. Much of their credibility rests on their ability to make a new sort of noise, for which they then can claim historical validation. The bottom line, as I never tire of saying, is that a great performance is a great performance, and it makes not a whit of difference if it's thoroughly traditional in conception or one that follows that latest HIP thinking. Interpretations that do the music justice will have more in common with each other for this very reason, never mind trivial variations in playing techniques or instrument construction.

Beethoven was a transitional figure. His early music tends to respond better to the current HIP approach than the more adventurous middle period or later works. For example, no great period instrument recordings exist of the Ninth Symphony, a piece that in many respects looks far into the future and sounds like nothing else of its time; nor any major HIP recordings of the concertos that feature the classical fortepiano or the baroque violin, although some noteworthy performances combine modern soloists with period instrument ensembles for accompaniment. Modern instruments evolved to overcome the obvious deficiencies of their earlier counterparts, and the superior results achieved by the great pianists and violinists who play them speak for themselves. When we get a violinist of the caliber of Jascha Heifetz playing Beethoven on a baroque violin, or we find the Martha Argerich of the fortepiano, then perhaps we'll have something to talk about. Until then, don't be fooled into believing that it's the instrument that makes the better performance.

In short, since the early nineteenth century, orchestral performance *standards* have changed markedly for the better, but performance *ideals*—not so much. This is because the actual music dictates both, and the most powerful voice driving this process remains Beethoven's.

The symphony orchestra must be accounted one of the greatest products of Western civilization, truly an extraordinary creation. We tend to take it for granted, assuming that some one hundred individuals, playing roughly a dozen and a half assorted types of instruments, come together and make beautiful music as a matter of course. We all too readily forget just how remarkable a thing it is. For Beethoven, however, the orchestra was still very much in the process of becoming its modern self. If not exactly a blank slate, a lot about it remained to be discovered and exploited. This he did with a daring, an imagination, and an uninhibited gusto unmatched to this day.

Beethoven's Dynamic Forms

Most listeners in Beethoven's day hadn't a clue about the details of musical forms and couldn't have cared less. Indeed, the ones that he used most frequently—the so-called sonata forms—were categorized only after his death by German musicologist Adolf Bernhard Marx (1795–1866), and not even Beethoven himself would have recognized many of the labels we attach today to the forms and methods that he adopted. As to audiences in the early nineteenth century, they listened much as we do now, point by point, tune by tune, except that they had no compunction about applauding the bits they liked and (ideally but not dependably) remaining silent at those they didn't. No one listened to "form" for its own sake, as a thing apart, and neither should you.

Why, then, do we bother talking about it? The main reason is because many different avenues lead to musical enjoyment, and a basic understanding of form certainly is one of them. It's an advantage we enjoy that Beethoven's contemporaries did not. Listeners in his day often found his orchestral music difficult because of its advanced style and personal—indeed, eccentric—manner of expression. It was both new and strange. Frequently, terrible performance standards didn't help the cause. Today that isn't so much an issue, but what does constitute a problem in our sensory-glutted world is the need to accept that it's OK to sit down for an hour or more, doing nothing but listening—that your sense of hearing provides you with all of the attention-grabbing entertainment value that you need to remain fully engaged and have a great time.

Once we've overcome this hurdle, something can be said for knowing what a symphony or a concerto is, why it sounds the way it does, and how to talk about it and share your enthusiasm knowledgeably. This, too, is information I propose to share in this chapter. What makes the topic particularly interesting is that, to a remarkable degree, our modern understanding of nineteenth-century musical form is not based on the average procedures of what the majority of composers were doing, but rather on the compositional practice of just one of them—Beethoven. Marx's theories represent a particularly obvious manifestation of this phenomenon. Beethoven's music was so compelling that he became both the theoretical standard and the practical model for everyone who came later. No one escaped his influence. That's quite something, isn't it?

As already mentioned, you probably will find this discussion more valuable if you've listened some on your own first. It's so much easier to understand a new concept if you have a sense, even a vague one, of what it is—even though you may not know technically what it's called. Imagine trying to describe the color red to a blind person, as opposed to the way children with normal vision usually learn it: they see a ripe apple, a barn, or a stop sign, and someone tells them, "That's red." To see it is to understand it. A seemingly impossible task thus can be accomplished almost instantaneously.

Although it's true that a structure moving through time, such as a piece of music, can't be explained in quite the same way as that red apple, the analogy still applies. To hear it is to understand it. As long as you can recognize something you've already heard, and notice whether it sounds the same or different when it reappears, you have all of the tools you need to understand the operation of musical form.

Let's begin with a definition. When we speak of "form" in traditional, tonal music, we mean *the use of time to focus and enhance expression*.

Think about a melody. If it's distinctive and captivating, you may want to hear it more than once and prolong the pleasure that it gives you. But how many times can you listen to it before it gets boring? Furthermore, what if some ways of playing the melody make it even more expressive and beautiful? Maybe it has the potential to reveal many different sides to its character or convey multiple shades of meaning. Perhaps it didn't sound so impressive at first listen but may become fabulous in a different context.

In order to take advantage of these possibilities, composers employ three basic techniques: *repetition*, *variation*, and *contrast*. All musical forms deploy these tactics to different degrees, and all of them necessarily take time. Once we understand this point, all we need to do is describe the individual recipes that the different forms adopt, adding the necessary terminology and nomenclature along the way. For now, we need only discuss in detail one type: *sonata form*. If I had to pick the single most important and influential invention in all of Western music, this would be it. However, it's more useful if we broaden our approach and call it the "sonata style," with the specific form representing one particularly potent manifestation of it. This, in any case, is the most useful way of thinking about the subject in Beethovenian terms, because he saw all of his music through this lens.

The sonata style offers a method for making purely instrumental music dramatic. It does this by allowing composers to create ideas—themes, motives, rhythms, chords, and textures—that function as characters in an unfolding dramatic framework, organizing them in a way that requires them to interact, evolve, and grow over the course of a movement, or even a whole, multi-movement piece. The music thus acquires a plot or narrative thread. Beethoven understood this concept better than any of his contemporaries, and he never lost sight of it as a compositional goal.

Keep in mind, however, that "drama" need not mean something sad or tragic in the colloquial sense that we often use the term today; it can be happy, or genuinely comic, and everything in between. Its emotional range is unlimited, but music being what it is, also inherently ambiguous. It's possible, in the absence of words, for the same idea to acquire multiple expressive meanings and even convey them simultaneously. This is not something we can describe verbally; it has to be experienced, but it gives instrumental music its richness and contributes to its repeatability. A great work never sounds quite the same way twice, and different performances illuminate its different facets.

I can think of no better way of illustrating this notion than with a visual analogy. Go to YouTube and look up the 1950s comedy sketch called "Argument to Beethoven's 5th" featuring Sid Caesar and Nanette

Fabray. The two characters mime a marital spat to an absolutely straight performance of the symphony's first movement. The genius lies in the fact that not only is the course of the fight perfectly easy to follow, but the music captures the couple's each and every gesture perfectly, right down to the movement of their hands. I have no hesitation in calling this one of the very greatest "interpretations" of Beethoven's Fifth ever preserved. Now, as we all know, this symphony, its first movement especially, is a very serious piece of music, so part of the sketch's humor undoubtedly stems from the cognitive dissonance that results from reducing its theoretically elevated musical language to the status of an ordinary domestic dispute. But the point is that the visual concept allows you to see as well as hear Beethoven's ability to create living characters enacting a dramatic scene through purely musical, nonverbal means. This is the sonata style in action.

One way we can be sure that a composer is working within the sonata style will be the presence of one or more sections, or separate movements, from a large work that adopts "sonata form." It is possible to describe this form several ways, and many versions of it are applicable to different musical genres. Beethoven's overtures, concertos, and symphonies each use proprietary brands of the sonata form, but all have certain important features in common. Over the years I have come up with a description that I believe will prove the most helpful to the majority of listeners. However, it pays to consider the advantages and disadvantages of the more standard definitions, especially for the useful terminology they introduce, and because you will see them mentioned often.

First, the basic, textbook definition of sonata form divides a movement into three principal sections: the *exposition* that presents the main themes (usually divided into a *first subject* and a *second subject*), the *development* that does stuff to them, and the *recapitulation*, which restates them. This formulation comes in handy for the names it gives a movement's principal parts, and we will use them in identifying specific passages. Other than that, however, it has the big disadvantage of giving the impression that each section has only two important themes and it exists only for one purpose. In reality, it may contain a limitless number of tunes, motives, and gestures, or they may come between the formal "subjects"; thematic development often can spread over the entire movement (or work), the sections can bleed into one another, and many movements, especially in Beethoven, feature lengthy introductions and (as we have already seen) codas that are as important as any of the other sections.

Second, another textbook definition views a movement in sonata form as "binary"—falling into two halves delineated by their harmonic functions.

The first half moves away from the principal tonality or key (called the tonic) to a new, closely related key set up in contrast to it. The reason for this is to convey the immediate impression of movement away from home in the initial statement of the main material, without going so far as to diminish the impact of later developments. You know that stuff is going to happen—just not exactly what. If this second, contrasting key lies a fifth above the tonic (i.e., five steps up on the scale that defines the home key), which is usual in pieces based in "major" tonalities, it is called the "dominant." So, in the tonic key of C major, the dominant is G major, and so forth. If the work adapts a minor key as its musical home base, then its secondary tonality will usually be the "relative major." This is the key that uses exactly the same notes as the primary, minor key, only it starts on a different part of the scale; and because of this slightly different arrangement, it sounds major. For example, E-flat major is the relative major key of C minor. C major is the relative major of A minor, and so forth.

The contrast between the major and minor modes in minor key-based works creates an additional level of contrast and tension that often makes such music sound more obviously emotional, or at least unstable, from the very start. However, bear in mind that composers can—and often do—suggest other possible keys during the initial presentation of thematic material. This is desirable as long as these alternative options do not firmly establish themselves and usurp the function of the ensuing development section, whose job it will be to explore them in depth. In other words, it's fine to talk about and plan taking a trip to some far-off destination before purchasing your plane ticket and going there.

This first half, then, corresponds to the exposition, and in classical period works it often is repeated to give you the chance to get the main material firmly into your memory and help you to notice how it develops later on.

In earlier times, the second half of the movement would be repeated as well, but Haydn, in his twelve "London" Symphonies, did away with this second-half repeat, effectively replacing it with a lengthy coda—a practice that Beethoven adopted with enthusiasm (as mentioned in the previous chapter). Otherwise, the second half of the movement, which contains the development and recapitulation, runs the themes through multiple keys and exploits their distance from the tonic to create an expressive intensity that only begins to be resolved when the music finds its way back to the home key at the start of the recapitulation. However, rather than moving (or "modulating") to a new, contrasting key as they did the first time around, all of the themes are modified so as to remain in, or keep returning to, the tonic and provide a satisfying feeling of finality.

The main advantage to this definition of sonata form is that it establishes the crucial concepts of "departure" and "return," alerting us that we should expect the music to describe actual *events* as it progresses. In short, it goes places, does things, and winds up back at home. The themes may be changed as a result of their experiences along the way, but always *recognizably*. Their evolution is both necessary and inevitable, and this is what gives music in sonata form its unique cogency, as well as that hard-to-describe, but easy-to-hear, organic feeling of expressive naturalness.

This is why it's such a pity that discussion of the underlying tonal and harmonic theory of sonata form often gets bogged down in academic technicalities that normal listeners won't understand and don't need to in order to make sense of what they are hearing. A movement's harmonic structure is not a goal in itself but a means to an end: namely, creating the dramatic framework that permits the various characters to act out their parts in a beautiful, intelligible way.

It's absolutely impossible to overstate the importance of regarding the tonic key as a musical "home base" and viewing different keys as "locations" of varying distance. The process of moving across that distance from one key to another (called "modulation") usually takes time. Not only does this give the sonata form its large scale as well as its propulsive energy, but it creates tension and arouses suspense as you listen. And consider another fascinating aspect: in a sonata form movement, you almost always know where you are. The rate of harmonic change and general feeling of stability tell you whether a passage belongs to the exposition (beginning), the development (middle), or the recapitulation/coda (end); and the better you get to know a piece of music, the clearer these subtleties become. Because a sonata movement effectively provides its own roadmap as it proceeds, it gratifies your expectations like no other musical form and makes listening an immensely satisfying experience.

Third, this brings us to my preferred description of a movement in sonata form, one based on the *kinds* of music it contains. These fall into two broad categories. First are the themes, motives, and chords that define a key as they are being played. You may not realize it, but every tune does this automatically as you hear it, sing it, or play it. Next is the music that takes us (and them) from one key to the next. For that reason, I call it "motion music." It may be every bit as melodically interesting and important as the official first and second subjects, and it can be quick or slow, loud or soft, or any of these in combination, but its purpose is to guide you to a different spot. In other words, it behaves differently. Beyond this basic observation, *all* of the ideas that we hear, of whatever kind, may qualify as "characters" in the unfolding drama. They even can swap jobs in a heartbeat.

That's really all there is to it. With a little practice, you will be able to recognize these two basic musical types with ease, especially in Beethoven, whose "motion music" does what the name suggests.

This approach has several advantages. In particular, it acknowledges that there are no limits to the number of themes or ideas that a "subject," and consequently a movement, can contain, or what they represent expressively. All that matters is how they function. For example, the first movement of Beethoven's Fifth Symphony contains two extremely distinctive themes as its first and second subjects. However, as Sid Caesar and Nanette Fabray hilariously demonstrate, this does not mean that these subjects represent two initially unrelated characters who only mix it up in the development section. They treat both ideas as dialogues, a concept that the structure and scoring of the themes' constituent musical phrases unquestionably supports.

Another advantage is that this conceptual framework also makes far better sense of what you hear than the textbook notion of two independent subjects separated by passages of transitional material. In the Fifth's first movement, the "motion music" is based entirely on the famous opening motive. It is thus a continuation, or ongoing "development" of the initial conversation, not a mechanical musical device designed merely to effect a change of key. On the other hand, in the slow movement of the Third Piano Concerto, the motion music is a totally independent, warm, elaborate theme for the strings that may well be the most beautiful and striking passage in the entire piece. It manages the necessary transition while remaining a unique, self-contained idea.

This ability of any character to step forward and assume a leading role is one factor that gives sonata form its endless range of possibilities. Within the boundaries established by the tonal framework that drives the music forward, just about anything can happen. The form's inherent flexibility also explains why, for instance, aside from a "family resemblance," no single Beethoven symphony sounds much like the others. Each is a unique creation with its own story to tell.

I call this chapter "Beethoven's Dynamic Forms" because not only did he invest the traditional, first movement sonata form with an extra jolt of energy, but he expanded the concept to embrace entire works by "sonatifying" their various movements—even those that adopt the different formal alternatives available at the time. These include the rondo, the simple ABA minuet or scherzo, sets of variations, and contrapuntal forms such as the fugue, all of which I will describe as we encounter them. Beethoven's sonata style embraces them all, conferring on large, multi-movement works a higher degree of unity and coherence as well as their characteristic excitement and drama.

In order to see how this works in practice, look at table 2.1, which gives an overview of the various movement forms that you will hear in the nine symphonies.

Right away you will notice that movements in sonata form overwhelmingly predominate, but what you don't see is that no two are exactly alike, or that all of the other formal types adopt some aspects of the sonata style as well. To appreciate that, we would have to discuss each example individually. I should also point out again that the three major categories of pieces examined in this book—overtures, concertos, and symphonies—use proprietary versions of sonata form, and we

Table 2.1. Beethoven Symphonies Movement Forms

Movement Number	I	II	III	IV	V
Symphony no. 1	Sonata	Sonata	ABA	Sonata	
Symphony no. 2	Sonata	Sonata	ABA	Rondo	
Symphony no. 3	Sonata	Rondo	ABA	Variations	
Symphony no. 4	Sonata	Rondo	ABABA	Sonata	
Symphony no. 5	Sonata	Variations	ABA	Sonata	
Symphony no. 6	Sonata	Sonata	ABABA	Sonata	Rondo
Symphony no. 7	Sonata	ABA	ABABA	Sonata	
Symphony no. 8	Sonata	Sonata	ABA	Sonata	
Symphony no. 9	Sonata	ABA	Variations	Variations	

will look at those as they arise. In the meantime, we have reached the moment where, in order to make sense of this theoretical discussion, we need to stop talking and start listening. So, let's take a detailed look at Beethoven's most iconic orchestral work, the complete Fifth Symphony, starting with a glance at some of its major recordings.

Symphony No. 5 in C Minor

Discography

Berlin Philharmonic Orchestra/Lorin Maazel
Lamoureux Orchestra/Igor Markevitch
Pittsburgh Symphony/Manfred Honeck
Vienna Philharmonic/Carlos Kleiber
Concertgebouw Orchestra/Erich Kleiber (mono)
Vienna Philharmonic/George Szell (Orfeo, live)
Philharmonia Orchestra/Otto Klemperer

The last time some of my colleagues and I made a survey of Beethoven's Fifth, in the late 1990s, more than 160 recordings were available.

Since then the number has only grown. No one can possibly have heard them all, and let's hope that no one is crazy enough to try. Suffice it to say, many, many very fine versions are available, including the ones in the complete symphony sets noted in part four. The recordings listed above are either highly acclaimed generally or personal favorites. You will note that none of them features period instruments. This is one of those works that (for me, anyway) just doesn't cut it when played with reduced forces using "historically informed" performance techniques, especially as regards the strings. The outer movements, in particular, simply need more weight and body than any of the extant period instrument ensembles provide.

First, let's talk about the classic version by the Kleibers, father (Erich) and son (Carlos). Both have similar virtues: superb ensemble, expressive directness, beautifully shaped slow movements, and an abundance of dramatic tension. Carlos Kleiber's version has been the reference performance for decades; and although it is just a bit impersonal for my taste, it's readily available, and you can't go wrong with it as a first choice. His father's performance features an especially noble account of the finale. George Szell was also a Beethoven Fifth specialist. He recorded it twice commercially in stereo, once in Cleveland, and again in Amsterdam with the Concertgebouw Orchestra. His live performance with the Vienna Philharmonic from the Salzburg Festival, however, might just be the best of all—a combination of power and poise seldom matched.

Otto Klemperer's Beethoven has lost some of its cachet since the period instrument folks took over. His second, stereo recording with the Philharmonia Orchestra, unusual in its day for including all of the repeats, remains one of the grimmest and (later) grandest available. Typically with this conductor, it also features a wealth of woodwind detail and a clarity of bass lines that you seldom will hear anywhere else. I don't find that Klemperer sounds slow once you're used to the basic speed, partly because the tempos he typically chooses for slow movements always flow, and because enough is going on in the quicker music to hold your attention. Something can be said for giving listeners a chance to absorb an especially gripping moment before moving on, but if you find the stereo version too much of a good thing, its slightly quicker mono predecessor awaits, still in very good sound.

The remaining three listings are personal favorites that fly under the radar, so to speak, but are well worth seeking out. Lorin Maazel's version was one of his earliest recordings, made when he was just beginning his career with the Deutsche Grammophon label. It has a freshness and intensity that his later recordings sometimes lacked. Igor Markevitch was a podium genius who brought a compelling combination of analytical clarity and theatrical flair to just about everything that he did. The Lamoureux Orchestra was one of the great French ensembles of the early 1960s, and its Beethoven is gloriously brassy, vibrant, and vivid. This version of the finale will knock your socks off. Finally, the partnership of Manfred Honeck and the Pittsburgh Symphony is one of the great musical happenings of the twenty-first century. Everything they do (so far) is worth hearing, including this take-no-prisoners account of the Fifth—guts and glory in equal measure, and exceptionally well-engineered.

Give the symphony a listen or three, and with at least some outstanding bits firmly in your mind, let's consider the musical nuts and bolts.

Scoring: piccolo, two flutes, two oboes, two clarinets, two bassoons, contrabassoon, two horns, two trumpets, three trombones, timpani, and strings.

This is one of only two symphonies that Beethoven wrote in minor keys (the other is the Ninth, in D minor). Controversy abounds as to whether individual keys have inherent emotional qualities, but many composers clearly had personal favorites, and they reserved them for specific kinds of expression. In particular, minor keys in our tradition have come to represent strong emotions of pathos, sadness, strife, anguish, pain, or despair, and many composers employ a "personal minor" whenever their music seeks to capture these feelings. Mozart's personal key was G minor. Haydn's was F minor. Beethoven's was C minor, the key of the Third Piano Concerto, the *Coriolan* Overture, the *Pathétique* Piano Sonata, and this symphony, among other pieces. Beethoven in C minor, as you are about to hear, is uniquely intense, turbulent, and brooding.

First Movement: Allegro con brio (Quickly with verve)
Track 5

Listen to that iconic opening, the symphony's famous four-note motto, but ask yourself: Just what is it? A motive? A theme? Motion music? The truth is that it's all of these, depending on how it's played—loud, soft, by the brass, strings, or winds; in unison, octaves, or harmonized; forcefully, timidly, quizzically, or pathetically. Does it represent one character, two as Caesar and Fabray suggest in their famous sketch, or perhaps even more? Would it help if I told you that although at first it sounds like a simple melody, Beethoven writes the agitated reply to the opening pronouncement as a dialog between three-part strings (first and second violins, and violas)? Even in this relatively short (about eight minutes) opening movement, Beethoven seems determined to exploit as many different possibilities for expression as he can.

The opening motive, then, quickly becomes a theme, and the theme morphs into a lengthy passage of motion music. Notice how each stage grows progressively longer. Although the movement itself is short, this process of continual expansion creates an impression of boundless energy and abundant space. It is also extremely developmental, revealing the opening gesture as capable of an organic feeling of growth and transformation. All of this occurs in the symphony's opening minute—well before we come to what passes technically for the "development section." In fact, the music moves forward with so much power that it almost misses its next stop. Beethoven slams on the brakes with a loud, grinding chord and immediately introduces the second subject with a bold horn call, also based on the four-note motive (with two added notes at the end). Keep this horn call in mind—it will become very important in a few minutes.

In some ways, the major key second subject is the opposite of the minor key first. Its initial phrases are lyrical and mellow, divided between violins and solo clarinet. Beethoven marks them "dolce" ("sweet"). There are three of them, eight notes each, but the violins continue the melody in four-note bits that add a greater sense of urgency as the next climax approaches. This passage will become the source of the most remarkable musical transformation in the entire movement. For now, it's interesting

Beethoven's Dynamic Forms

to note that whereas the first subject's nervous energy makes it want to expand, the more relaxed second subject shows a tendency to contract, breaking into smaller pieces. If you listen carefully, you can hear the lower strings continuing to mutter the symphony's opening motto throughout. A typically Beethovenish crescendo then introduces more motion music in the full orchestra, closing the exposition with a return to the opening motto and so leading either back to the beginning or onward into the development section.

Until about 1960, many recordings of Beethoven's symphonies left out the exposition repeats, but from then on it has become increasingly normal to include them (the *Eroica*, due to its exceptional length, remains a special case). There is no right way. Leaving them out tends to emphasize the tripartite view of a movement as having three main sections, whereas including the repeats gives them a more "binary" feel—that is, of having two halves of roughly the same length: the repeated exposition in the first half, the development plus recapitulation in the second. I usually prefer to hear the repeat for a couple of reasons, not the least of which is because you get to experience some really great music twice.

That said, you might argue quite reasonably that a literal repeat contradicts the sensation of forward movement that the sonata form creates, and in some instances this might be true, particularly in later romantic pieces. However, music operates by its own set of rules, and I find that including the repeat just as often effectively highlights the dramatic developments that follow. This is surely the case in Beethoven's Fifth Symphony, where the first movement otherwise is quite short. You might want to consider listening to it both ways—easy to do with a compact disc—to see if either approach gives you the greater satisfaction.

We have now reached the development section, which opens with the initial motto and first subject, although clearly in a different key (or location). The main theme attempts to engage in civilized conversation between the strings and woodwinds but gets swept away by a blast of rage from the full orchestra. The horn call that introduced the second subject then stages an intervention and tries to seize control—you may just hear the woodwinds continuing to mutter bits of the main theme underneath. This diverts the argument onto an entirely new path, losing energy in the process, first becoming a heavy, two-note dialogue between strings and winds, then a spacey, one-note pulsation, among the lightest of all Beethoven's "bounce" ideas. A loud interruption by the horn call (played by violins, actually) tries to force the music back on track but fails. Suddenly the first subject crashes in, seemingly from all sides at once. Before you know it, we're back in C minor, and the recapitulation has arrived.

The most important thing to bear in mind about recapitulations, especially Beethoven's, is that the return of the original material need not be literal. Indeed, because sonata form requires restatement of the second subject in the home key, it *cannot* be literal. Both the motion music and the second subject itself need to be recomposed, and even the first subject can be recast to take it in new directions. In this case, the opening theme has sounded forceful when loud, agitated when soft, and now, by adding a moving little solo for the oboe, Beethoven introduces an entirely new and surprising degree of pathos. It doesn't last long, however, and you can hear clearly how the loud chords at the end of motion music are altered to keep the second subject in the home key of C (major in this case).

Now comes a very famous bit of Beethoven Fifth trivia. The horn call that formerly introduced the second subject instead is played by the bassoon, because horns in Beethoven's day needed more time than he allows to be able to play in different keys. They had differing lengths of tubing, called "crooks," that the player could insert to give the instrument the required notes (now they have keyed valves); but partially disassembling the instrument, retuning, and getting warmed up and ready to play is seldom practical in the midst of a movement—hence the bassoon, which many listeners find comical in comparison to the horn. Because of this obvious technical problem, until recently many conductors rescored this passage for the modern horn, which has no problem playing it, arguing that this is what Beethoven clearly would have preferred. I personally agree. The modern fad for "authenticity," however, frowns on this liberty, a fact that gladdens the hearts of bassoonists everywhere, assuming they can play the passage without making it sound silly (it can be done).

Meanwhile, back in the recapitulation, you may have noticed that the pathetic little oboe solo added to the first theme, combined with the revamped motion music and more lightly scored second subject, tend to weaken the overall impression that the music made the first time around. There's a reason for this. Beethoven has no intention of ending the movement at this point. He's saving the best for last: the coda. Now he whips up a fury that's truly unprecedented in the history of orchestral music. The most amazing thing about it is that it's not based on the first subject at all, although it begins that way with an outburst that's part hysterical (full orchestra), part quizzical (the bassoon again).

Recall that back in the development section, Beethoven only used the second subject's introductory horn call. What follows now is a transformation of the entire tune so dramatic that you might not recognize it at first. However, if you paid attention to the melody's latter half, where it is broken into four-note phrases, you will have no trouble recognizing them in the ferocious vortex of sound that Beethoven unleashes, initially in the strings, then in dialogue between the strings and everyone else. The emotional effect of this is twofold. Not only is it the most violent passage in the entire movement, but in a devastating about-face it wrenches that formerly sweet second subject over to the "dark side" once and for all. Having accomplished its evil plan, the opening motto can return one last time in a gesture of supreme power, to which the woodwinds add a helpless shrug.

The transformation of the second subject from a serene and lyrical melody to a psychotic nightmare is an especially extreme example of what the sonata style can accomplish. Most music of this kind, including Beethoven's, is joyous and only sporadically troubled. Indeed, the Fifth Symphony will conclude with one of the most triumphant finales ever written. It has as large a range of positive emotions as of negative ones. What makes the sonata style and its associated forms so uniquely powerful is their ability to contain such wide-ranging contrasts within a structure at once severely logical but also wholly natural sounding. A great sonata movement will never strike you as contrived. Its form and content are inseparable.

Second Movement: Andante con moto (Walking pace, with movement) Track 6

I hesitate to speculate about what specific emotions the first movement may describe ("fate" is a popular choice), preferring to focus on what it does. Suffice it to say, the piece set a new world record for music of uncompromising, obsessive grimness, and for that reason it's especially interesting to discover how Beethoven responds to the extreme emotional situation he has just presented. The answer, in this case, is an act of escapism—a moment of respite that forms a complete contrast to what we've just heard. However, because the four movements that belong to this symphony constitute a complete whole, some elements must tie the second movement into the discourse initiated by the first. We'll get to them momentarily.

This Andante is a set of variations but one completely original in shape. Some commentators say it has two themes that alternate, but you can also make the argument, because they begin with the same rhythm and sound closely related, that it is really just one large idea, with the alleged "second theme" merely a grander, marchlike continuation of the first. Beethoven scores the first theme for cellos and violas, and the second for woodwinds and strings, culminating in a bold, brassy fanfare in C major, the ultimate goal of the entire symphony. Between the two main ideas is transitional material, and a mysterious concluding passage after the second one that ends with a bounce. These are varied, too. In short, I find it simpler to think of the entire, four-part complex (theme 1—transition—theme 2—codetta or "little coda") as a unit, because that's how Beethoven treats it, at least initially. The main breaks between variations come only after both themes have been heard in succession.

This, then, is the initial setup. When listening to any piece in variation form, the most important thing to grasp is the shape of the main theme(s). The actual structure of this movement consists of a first presentation of the main theme complex, two variations of the whole thing in which the first tune speeds up and the second remains relatively unchanged, then a long coda based mostly on the first theme, initially in a quirky, minor-key version given to the woodwinds, then grandly in the full orchestra. The ending—a loud one, unusual in a slow movement (although both Haydn and Beethoven liked the effect)—uses the transition melody, which, like everything else, is based on the same initial rhythm as both principal themes, or half-themes, or whatever you want to call them. Either way, the movement is just wonderfully tuneful and original.

Some of the music's special character stems from its main key: A-flat major. This requires a bit of explanation, so please bear with me. A-flat major is the "subdominant" of E-flat major, the key in which the first movement's second subject first appeared. A subdominant key starts with the note a fifth below the tonic (that's the "sub" part), which in this case is E-flat. If the major-key second subject of the first movement already was a moment of lyrical repose, then all you need to know about subdominant harmony is that it sounds even more relaxed. Indeed, heard in context, with an appropriate melody as the messenger of expression, it has a definitely mellow, even autumnal quality.

This, by the way, is about as far as I'm willing to go on the subject of key relationships and their audible effects. As you get to know this music well, and read more about it in concert program notes or recording booklets, you may hear many claims about the long-term formal significance of this or that note or passage in a particular key. I'm not sure I believe them. No one knows how far tonal memory extends in real time, and it surely differs greatly from one person to the next. Many claims about the expressive meaning of key relationships, although they sound terribly learned and definitive, are mere speculation based on no demonstrable facts. Wagner, in his *Ring* operas, begins in E-flat major and ends there four *days* later, but I wouldn't expect anyone to notice. I don't feel comfortable pushing the issue beyond passages or sections a few minutes apart at most—perhaps longer if you can keep some especially telling bits of a work firmly in mind while the rest plays.

Beethoven places his Andante, then, in exactly the right key to emphasize its otherworldly character without making it sound completely foreign. You may or may not realize this consciously, and it doesn't matter, because the contrast manifests itself simply by paying attention to the various musical ideas. It could be that for some listeners the triumphant pageant in the finale, when it finally arrives, sounds more fulfilling because it shares the same key as the heroic brass fanfare from the Andante; but many other factors are at work that are equally, if not more important, including Beethoven's treatment of dynamics, scoring, and texture. He never puts all of his musical eggs in one basket. In any case, it will be the job of the next two movements to make a reality of what, for now, only appears as an initial promise.

Scherzo: Allegro Track 7

The symphonic scherzo (the word means "joke" in Italian) was Beethoven's invention. As a successor to the minuet of the classical period, the scherzo basically is a dance piece in triple time, often in simple, ABA form. Both the "A" and "B" sections fall into two halves, both repeated, and for a historical reason that no one knows for sure, the central "B" section is called a "Trio." Beethoven often modified this basic plan, perhaps most originally in the movement under consideration here. Nothing could be less dance-like. The music is alternately spooky and stern. The "A" section has no big repeats, but there's much more to this music than that. For example, as everyone who has heard this symphony since its premiere has noticed, the loud theme in the horns that immediately follows the creepy opening employs the symphony's initial, four-note motto. That makes the relationship between the two movements extra clear, as does the fact that the Scherzo returns to the first movement's home key of C minor.

Has Beethoven then ignored the Andante entirely and only resumed the earlier conversation here? Not at all. Some commentators have pointed out a brief moment where the four-note motto appears in the Andante—I leave it to you to find it. Others maintain that this is mere coincidence, and I agree with them. Beethoven's true method of explaining how the Andante fits into the overall scheme is perhaps less obvious but even more cogent.

Remember, we noticed that the main theme of the second movement has two halves, a lyrical tune for lower strings featuring "dotted" rhythms (dum, dadum, dadum, etc.), followed by a march. Well, this scherzo does exactly the same thing. The main theme has two themes, or two halves, depending on how you feel them. The first is played by

Beethoven's Dynamic Forms

cellos and basses in similarly dotted rhythms, answered by a transitional phrase in the violins and woodwinds, exactly as in the Andante. Because the tempo is quicker, this all happens much faster than before, but the concept still is the same.

Next comes a march, again as in the previous movement, only this march features the first movement's opening motto. The Scherzo's first theme may sound vaguely related to what we just heard in the Andante, whereas the second tune is melodically entirely different but, as a march, similar in *kind*. This is what gives the "A" section of the Scherzo the kind of sinister, hallucinatory, half-remembered quality that makes it so gripping. It combines the structure of the Andante's theme(s) with the key, and some of the melodic content, of the first movement.

In the classical period, the minuet traditionally was a point of relaxation, a diverting interlude standing somewhat outside the more rigorous, ongoing symphonic discourse. Haydn began the process of integrating all of the movements of a symphony into a unified whole; and in pieces such as this Scherzo, Beethoven completed the job. Nothing is "off topic" about this music, and its centrality to the symphony's overall plan only will become more obvious in the finale.

That's not to say that the music is devoid of contrast, or even humor. We find both in the trio, or "B" section. This is a *fugato*, a contrapuntal episode in which the parts come in one by one at staggered intervals, but they don't continue to develop contrapuntally as they would in a formal fugue. In fact, the joke here is that the music rises from the bottom of the basses to the top of the violins but otherwise goes nowhere. The initial entry has been an acid test for orchestral bass sections since Beethoven's day. Early performances in France (and probably elsewhere) simply left out the bass part and let the cellos do all of the work.

Each half of this section is repeated, and the humor increases at the opening of the second half, as the basses only get going after a couple of false starts. The overall mood is rough and jolly, but Beethoven writes out the second-half repeat so that it evaporates gradually and leads back to the Scherzo's main section, now reduced to a mere skeleton of its former self. Prominent writing for the bassoon and pizzicato (plucked) strings, with flecks of woodwind color barely managing to suggest the once-fearsome march tune, turn the music into a ghostly procession that gradually sinks into total darkness. Timpani softly pound out the four-note motto over sustained strings, becoming a steady throbbing pulse, while the violins rise in slow waves that ignite a huge crescendo leading directly into the

Finale: Allegro Track 8

Changing key to a triumphant C major, Beethoven now pulls out all of the stops. He adds three trombones, piccolo, and a contrabassoon to the orchestra for the first time in the work (the contrabassoon likely was chugging along on the bass line all along, but never mind). The opening brass fanfare might remind you of the similar music in the Andante, as well it should. What sounded there like the mere promise of victory finally has materialized as a grand movement in full sonata form, complete with repeated exposition. Until recently the repeat very rarely was heard, but now it's pretty common—at least on recordings, if not always in live performances.

The first subject consists of a joyous hubbub of fanfares, rushing scales, and some vigorous bouncing and jumping about. Pay special attention to the transitional "motion music" in the horns and woodwinds, with its difficult-to-hear answer in the basses. Beethoven often puts interesting material in the depths of the orchestra during loud passages, leaving the conductor the task of achieving clarity without losing power. That horn tune is glorious, and it will become the basis for the coda. The second subject features a theme incorporating many repetitions of the symphony's four-note motto rhythm, now turned into a dialogue between the full orchestra and the softer strings. This leads to still another tune in slower tempo, first on woodwinds, then answered by the full orchestra, that also will return in the coda. It rises to a big climax that either leads back to the beginning for the exposition repeat, or onward into the development section.

Although the various components of a sonata exposition are all clearly in place, the general impact of this music is very different than it was in the first movement. The abundance of material combined with the energy of its presentation produces the effect of a triumphant procession. It's almost like watching a parade: one colorful float after another passes by, accompanied by brass bands and other entertaining diversions. There's no attempt at subtlety, nor any strong emotional contrast. It's all pure, physical joy.

The development section has one main purpose: purge the symphony's four-note motto of any negative connotations. Accordingly, it begins by presenting variants of the second subject. As the level of excitement increases, the three rising notes of the movement's initial fanfare (plus one preliminary note for emphasis) appear on the trombones, alternating with the motto hammered out by the rest of the orchestra. This battle between opposing forces lunges headfirst into a positively manic pileup of sonority, getting louder and louder, straining to the utmost, until the whole thing snaps like a rubber band, and the violins retreat in a sudden decrescendo.

What comes next is one of the most talked about passages in Western music for what it does both formally and expressively. The march from the Scherzo returns furtively, timidly, revealing the third and fourth movements to be an unbroken whole. However, the effect of this return has an entirely different meaning than it did when the Scherzo's march first appeared. Initially, it was bold but grim, then ghostly. Now, after all of this C major shouting and celebrating, the effect is akin to shining a bright light into a corner of a dark basement and realizing that all of the ominous shapes and shadows were nothing more than common household items gathering dust. The symphony's four-note motto has been completely defanged and rendered harmless within the context of the massive victory party that surrounds it.

As soon as we realize this, another big crescendo initiates the recapitulation. This proceeds regularly, in the same order as before, except that at what should be the end of whole process Beethoven combines the motive of the opening fanfare from the development section with the main idea of the second subject—the one based on the motto—turning the whole into a single melody. In other words, the four-note motto isn't just neutralized; it is integrated into the joyful melodic flow. With this accomplished, the music comes to a partial halt, and the "coda that just won't quit" begins. This is based on two ideas that remained unexploited to this point: the transitional "motion music" between the main subjects and the exposition's closing theme, now speeded up from its relatively stately initial presentation and turned into a mad dash to the finish line.

The principle at work here is less a function of the sonata style than of what later became known as the symphonic ideal: the idea that all of the material in a movement should contribute to the music's expressive goal and be pressed into service for this purpose. In other words, despite the exuberant outpouring of thematic material in this finale, and its more generous proportions as compared to the incredibly terse, no-nonsense first movement, it contains not a single gratuitous note. It accomplishes the twin jobs of being both formally self-sufficient and neatly summarizing and providing a fitting conclusion to the entire symphony.

In shifting the weight of the main expressive argument onto the finale, Beethoven created an entirely new type of symphony, one that had incalculable impact on later, romantic music. The "tragedy to triumph" topic in minor-key symphonies became almost a cliché. Within Beethoven's own output, this progression remains atypical. All of his other symphonies without exception, even the Ninth, respect the classical practice that reserves the most sophisticated formal and expressive subtleties for their first movements, with the remaining ones revealing a progressive tendency to employ less complex structures that convey emotion and meaning more simply, if not less energetically. This is even more evident in the concertos, with their often very long first movements followed by two shorter ones.

The Fifth, then, is in some respects an atypical piece, and yet for this very reason it represents a perfect specimen of the sonata style in action, in particular its ability to help the composer craft large works with their own very distinctive personalities. This "Infinite Diversity in Infinite Combinations," which *Star Trek* fans will recognize as the mainspring of Vulcan philosophy, lies at the heart of Beethoven's method.

Let me conclude this discussion of form with an entertaining cautionary tale from the Fifth's reception history.

It is a mistake to assume that his contemporaries allegedly working within the same musical school fully understood what Beethoven was about. Most did not. Consider the comments of Louis Spohr on

Beethoven's Fifth. Spohr (1784–1859) became one of the most famous and frequently performed German symphonists in the first half of the nineteenth century. He composed ten symphonies in all, a couple of which turn up on concert programs today, albeit infrequently. All of them have been recorded multiple times. He also was an important conductor who promoted Beethoven's music despite his personal reservations. Here is what Spohr wrote in his autobiography about the Fifth:

> Though with many individual beauties, yet it does not constitute a classical whole. For instance, the introductory theme of the very first passage is wanting in that dignity which according to my feeling the commencement of a Symphony should of a necessity possess. Setting this aside, the short and easily comprehended theme, certainly permits of being carried out very thematically, and is combined also by the composer with the other principal ideas of the first subject in an ingenious and effective manner. The Adagio in A flat is in part very fine, yet the same passages and modulations repeat themselves much too frequently, and although always with richer ornamentation, become in the end wearisome. The Scherzo is highly original, and of real romantic coloring, but the Trio with the noisy running bass is to my taste much too rough. The concluding passage with its unmeaning noise, is the least satisfactory; nevertheless the return to the Scherzo at this part is so happy an idea, that the composer may be envied for it. Its effect is most captivating! But what a pity that this impression is so soon obliterated by the returning noise!

As you can plainly see, either Spohr is not interested in the niceties of the sonata style, or he feels his readers would not know what he is talking about should he refer to them. More to the point, although Spohr speaks of a "classical whole," whatever that is, he plainly has no conception of the Fifth as an "individual whole"—a unique work that fulfills all of the expectations it creates and operates according to a consistent set of aesthetic principles. He judges each moment as it comes, according to his personal taste, separate and apart from its function within the larger organism. The return of the Scherzo in the finale's development section is "captivating" because it's unexpected, not because it represents the fulfillment of an expressive journey that has been in progress from the symphony's very first note.

The moral of the story is this: As listeners, we are entitled to like some bits of a work better than others, but we stand a much better chance of understanding and enjoying the whole thing if we don't insist that the piece would be better off without its alleged disagreeable moments. In other words, nothing in Beethoven happens without a purpose, and if you approach the music keeping this thought in mind, his forms largely will take care of themselves.

Part 2

Overtures

Discography (listed by orchestra/conductor)

Tonhalle Orchestra of Zurich/David Zinman
Boston Symphony Orchestra/Charles Munch
Lamoureux Orchestra/Igor Markevitch
NBC Symphony Orchestra/Arturo Toscanini
Philharmonia Orchestra/Otto Klemperer
Minnesota Orchestra/Stanislaw Skrowaczewski
Cleveland Orchestra/George Szell

Although discs are available that contain Beethoven overture collections, you're just as likely to find them as fillers to performances of the individual symphonies; and because they tend not to appear singly (unless you opt to receive music via digital downloads or streaming services), purchasing various albums invariably involves duplication of content. You'll just have to check as you go and see what combinations strike your fancy. This isn't necessarily a bad thing, because Beethoven's music

Overtures: Orchestration (in addition to strings and timpani)

Title	flutes	piccolo	oboes	clarinets	bassoons	contrabassoon	horns	trumpets	trombones
Prometheus	2		2	2	2		2	2	
Leonore no. 2	2		2	2	2		4	3	3
Leonore no. 3	2		2	2	2		4	3	3
Coriolan	2		2	2	2		2	2	
Leonore no. 1	2		2	2	2		4	2	
Egmont	2	1	2	2	2		4	2	
The Ruins of Athens	2		2	2	2		4	2	
King Stephen	2		2	2	2	1	4	2	
Fidelio	2		2	2	2		4	2	2
Namensfeier	2		2	2	2		4	2	
The Consecration of the House	2		2	2	2		4	2	3

Part 2: Overtures

so clearly benefits from a variety of interpretive approaches, and you'll doubtless enjoy having more than just one of your favorites.

Both the David Zinman and Stanislaw Skrowaczewski collections feature all eleven pieces in this category, the former adopting elements of "historically informed" style but with a full-size modern orchestra—in other words, the best of both worlds. Skrowaczewski was a marvelous conductor, and his two-CD set, if you can find it, originally appeared at budget price. The performances are as bold and exciting as you could want. *The Consecration of the House* really sizzles, and the dissonant explosion at the end of *Leonore* no. 3 will send you running for cover. Additional overture collections by Kurt Masur (complete, with the Leipzig Gewandhaus Orchestra) and Claudio Abbado (eight, with the Vienna Philharmonic) aren't bad. They will do in a pinch, but also don't make any special claims on your attention or your purse.

Another well-known complete overture collection is not included in the above list: Herbert von Karajan's with the Berlin Philharmonic. For all of the beauty of the playing, Karajan's preference for smoothness and blend, his tendency to downplay important woodwind parts, often strikes me as contrary to the spirit of the music. I mention him because you may find his set readily available. It always has been well promoted, so if you're curious, feel free to sample it and draw your own conclusions. I confess that I sometimes enjoy it as a kind of decadent indulgence for its sheer richness of timbre and magnificent string sound, but only in limited quantities.

Otto Klemperer and George Szell both recorded almost all of the Beethoven overtures, some of them multiple times: Klemperer in his typically grand, gritty, unsentimental style; Szell, razor-sharp, lean, and always exciting. You can't go wrong with either. As you might already have noticed from the discussion in chapter 1, Beethoven in the French manner has its own claims to legitimacy, authenticity even, and that tradition—crisp, clear, timbrally colorful, and elegant without blandness—shines through proudly in the brilliant performances led by Markevitch and Munch.

Finally, Toscanini's Beethoven basically defined the composer for two generations of listeners in the first half of the twentieth century. His NBC Symphony album contains six overtures, including thrilling accounts of *Leonore* no. 3, *Coriolan*, and *The Consecration of the House*, which was a genuine rarity when Toscanini got his hands on it in 1947. In general, I am not a fan of "historical" recordings as such (these are taken from mono radio broadcasts from the 1930s and '40s) because they include virtually nothing that you can't hear done equally well in superb modern sound; but these performances are listenable and, more important, they are special: iconic examples of what became the modern standard in powerful, idiomatic Beethoven interpretation.

Theatrical Overtures

Prometheus
Leonore no. 1
Egmont
The Ruins of Athens
King Stephen
Fidelio

Everyone loves a good overture. Beethoven wrote eleven of them, some for actual theatrical productions, some for the concert hall, and a few that began as the former but wound up as the latter. All of them are performed today purely as concert pieces, with the exception of the overture to *Fidelio*, which is played both independently and in tandem with its eponymous opera. Is there any formal difference between the two types? Well, yes, but it's not a hard-and-fast rule. With the exception of *Prometheus* and *Coriolan*, all of them employ what we might call "theatrical" scoring: that is, four horns and the possibility of further extras: an additional trumpet, trombones, piccolo, or contrabassoon.

Those extra horns wouldn't join the orchestra of the symphonies until the Ninth, even though the doubling of wind parts in large ensembles was not unusual, but from the scoring of the overtures alone we learn two important facts: First, theater orchestras were larger and probably more accomplished than the small, private orchestras in aristocratic homes or the pickup ensembles Beethoven had access to otherwise. Second, to the extent that the symphonies make use of some or all of these luxury instrumental additions, the theater is where Beethoven found them. Indeed, Beethoven's orchestral music set new standards of both colorfulness and theatricality, whether or not intended for the stage.

In addition to unusually full scoring, most of the overtures employ a proprietary version of sonata form. All of them start with slow introductions, and all of them avoid repeating their expositions. Instead of the usual development section, in the theatrical overtures listed above we find a brief transition, an independent episode, or a return to the original introduction leading straight into the recapitulation. As you can hear at your leisure, each work features its own version of this strategy. By the way, Beethoven didn't invent it. You often find something similar in Mozart's opera overtures and serenades (check out *The Marriage of Figaro*).

The reasons for these formal conventions become clear after a moment's thought. An overture is merely an introduction to something bigger and more important. Its opening should seize the listener's attention—a slow, grand introductory passage does just that—whereas the main body of the work must entertain without requiring any especially intense intellectual effort. The overture also may suggest the atmosphere or setting of the drama that inspired it—and this suggestion or foreshadowing of external events has real formal consequences. Two of these are the omission of exposition repeats and the minimal gestures toward development. These also mean that, as at least regards the theatrical overtures, their duration is relatively brief when compared to roughly contemporaneous symphonic, sonata-form first movements.

Consider these timings of performances by the same conductor and orchestra (David Zinman and the Tonhalle Orchestra of Zurich):

Overtures	**Symphony First Movements**
Prometheus: 4:48	Symphony no. 1: 7:58
Leonore no. 1: 8:56	*Eroica* Symphony: 15:34
Egmont: 7:25	Symphony no. 4: 9:59
The Ruins of Athens: 4:19	*Pastoral* Symphony: 10:21
King Stephen: 6:29	Symphony no. 7: 13:25
Fidelio: 6:08	Symphony no. 8: 8:14

Theatrical Overtures

Most of the pieces in this group, then, generally are classed as "light," or in any event "lighter" Beethoven—some deliberately so on his part; others, well, we're not quite so sure about his ultimate intentions, but they are no less enjoyable for that. However, among the six indisputable theatrical overtures is one major exception. For *Egmont*, written to a tragedy by Germany's greatest literary figure, Johann Wolfgang von Goethe, Beethoven composed one of his most powerful short works. This was the piece chosen to be performed at the memorial service for the Israeli athletes killed by terrorists at the 1972 Munich Olympics, and it expresses as effectively as any music can both doom-laden turbulence and, ultimately, heroic striving. Let's begin this survey, then, by taking a closer listen to *Egmont*.

In case you were wondering, Goethe's play is a tragedy, which means an unhappy ending in which the hero usually dies. His girlfriend in this case, Clärchen, dies as well (to some very affecting music, as it turns out). What attracted Beethoven to the subject is that the protagonists die fighting oppression, a topic that always excited his passionate attention. Egmont's struggle for justice is so heroic and noble that his death for a good cause inspired Beethoven to conclude his music for the play with a "Victory Symphony," and these two minutes of orchestral celebration occupy most of the coda to the overture as well. The reason it sounds like a completely independent episode is because that's exactly what it is.

Egmont's coda might sound perfectly satisfying as it stands, but ultimately its justification is extramusical: it refers specifically to the plot. The music's sudden switch from minor-key turmoil to major-key euphoria is very exciting in terms of contrast, but it is expressively unmotivated. Beethoven's symphonic codas can and do introduce new ideas and contrasting feelings from time to time, but none of them consists of little else. In a symphony, as opposed to an overture, all of the most important events arise from within the self-contained universe of the work's thematic material, without reference to external sources. But we are getting ahead of ourselves.

Despite its comparative simplicity, the form of the *Egmont* Overture is ingenious and incredibly gripping in performance. Let me map it out for you (Track 1):

Introduction: two ideas, A and B

Exposition: First Subject (B); Second Subject (A), in the main allegro tempo

Transition: B, from the introduction but in the main tempo, leading back to:

Recapitulation: First Subject (B); Second Subject (A), with minor enrichments

Coda: A, as transition to the concluding "Victory Symphony"

As you can see, the entire overture evolves out of the introduction's two principal ideas. Beethoven simply speeds them up and plays them in reverse order in crafting his formal exposition, and he uses them individually to make his transitions. Very exciting motion music featuring swift, rising-scale patterns moves us from one location to the next. You should pay attention to these gestures, too: they are characteristic, Beethovenian "fingerprints" found also in the second movement and finale of the Fifth Symphony, and in the Seventh's first movement introduction.

None of this formal cleverness would matter if it were not placed in the service of some very arresting thematic ideas. As the roadmap above shows, the introduction contains two of them. Theme "A," which, speeded up, will become the overture's second subject, consists of solemn, rhythmic string chords alternating with plaintive woodwind responses. Theme "B," sung out initially by the violins and solo woodwinds above a gently agitated accompaniment, is a simple, six-note fragment that tries to become an ominous descending scale, only succeeding when the cellos take over and carry it forward as the overture's dark, doom-laden first subject. This process is varied and repeated in the transition back to the recapitulation; "A," blasted out by the horns and (eventually) trumpets plus timpani in the coda, leads to the final "Victory Symphony."

You will notice, then, that despite the ostensibly "lighter" version of sonata form that *Egmont* employs, the music hardly suffers from a lack of development. In a very real sense, except for that "Victory Symphony" at the end, the overture is *all* development, and that is why so often it's not helpful to try to squeeze the music into textbook notions of structure. Much of the emotional intensity and urgent power we feel in listening to *Egmont* comes from its extraordinary thematic cohesion and focus on the ongoing evolution of just a few distinctive ideas—in other words, from the expressive impact of the truly organic development that takes place outside of the section traditionally reserved for that purpose.

In fact, Beethoven's music for Goethe's play is so compelling that it's fair to say that more people probably know of *Egmont* from the overture than from reading or seeing the original drama, which never has been viewed as one of Goethe's better efforts. Music has the ability to do that; in this case, Beethoven has packed into seven or eight minutes enough action to render the next three hours of spoken theater practically unnecessary. That this admirable quality isn't always the right thing in all circumstances is a lesson that Beethoven eventually would learn in trying to find the ideal overture to his single opera, *Fidelio* (originally called *Leonore*).

For that work, Beethoven wrote no less than four overtures before finding one that both lived up to his musical standards and didn't completely obliterate the relatively sunny and inconsequential first act of the opera. In listening to them, it helps to know the plot to understand better the challenge that Beethoven faced when writing the overtures. Leonore's husband, Florestan, is being held as a political prisoner by Don Pizarro, the regional governor. Disguised as a young man named Fidelio, Leonore infiltrates the jail where he is being held to locate and free him, which she does by holding Pizarro at pistol point as the king's minister arrives in the nick of time. That's basically the whole story, and all of the good stuff happens in the second act, which takes place mostly in Florestan's subterranean dungeon cell. The first act offers an hour of domestic comedy: Fidelio has to deal with the amorous intentions of Marzelline, daughter of Rocco, the jailer.

This bifurcated plotline caused Beethoven, who was hugely inspired by Leonore's devotion and heroism, no end of trouble in trying to decide what the opera's overture should do. Should it attempt to mirror the drama as a whole and capture the larger message of freedom and liberation from darkness, simply provide an apt introduction to the much lighter first act, or do a little bit of both? Two of the overtures, *Leonore* nos. 2 and 3, try the first option, the *Fidelio* Overture adopts the second, and the *Leonore* Overture no. 1 combines elements of both approaches. These latter two works qualify as "theatrical" as we define the form for our purposes here. We will look more closely at the *Leonore* Overtures nos. 2 and 3 in the next chapter.

The overture to *Fidelio* was the last of the four to be written. It is the shortest of the bunch, and like *Egmont*, the outward simplicity of form belies great sophistication in its execution. The ostensibly slow introduction begins with an energetic orchestral fanfare in quicker tempo, immediately repeated, that will evolve into the principal theme of the allegro. The exposition is "monothematic": that is, it contains no independent second subject and no development section. Everything evolves out of the main theme, and the coda begins with a return to the music of the introduction. The overture does not directly quote any music from the opera, but Beethoven very subtly and effectively links it to the drama by featuring, both in the introduction and ensuing allegro, the noble timbre of the French horn, which also characterizes so much of the music to come.

The *Leonore* Overture no. 1 initially was the source of much confusion among Beethoven scholars. It was actually the third to be written, in 1807, for a possible production of the opera in Prague that never materialized. The very high opus number (138) reflects the fact that it was only discovered among Beethoven's papers after his death, at which time scholars believed that it represented his first attempt. It is still the least frequently heard of the four opera overtures, perhaps because it has neither the energetic brevity of that for *Fidelio* nor the overwhelming impact of *Leonore* nos. 2 and 3. Nonetheless, it's a very attractive work whose most outstanding feature is the central Adagio that takes the place of the development section. This is based on the tune of Florestan's big act two aria "In des Lebens Frühlingstagen" ("In the springtime of life"). This same melody features prominently in the other two *Leonore* overtures, and it's very enjoyable to hear all three pieces and make comparisons among them while following Beethoven on the journey to *Fidelio*, his final conception of what the right operatic overture should be.

Next up: *The Ruins of Athens* and *King Stephen*. Most great composers have moments of lesser inspiration or find themselves pressured by a deadline to compromise quality. That's how these two pieces often are described, not entirely without reason. *The Ruins of Athens*, in particular, is Beethoven's shortest overture and clearly the least substantial in other ways as well. Probably the best thing about it is its atmospheric introduction, which quotes a couple of the vocal numbers to come, and the big central crescendo that serves as the transition back to the first subject of the Allegro. The work is formally truncated: it simply stops after the recapitulation of the energetic first theme, which in any case isn't one of Beethoven's more memorable ideas. The much more charming second subject, a duet for oboe and bassoon over pizzicato (plucked) strings, never comes back. Also, it has no coda, a sure sign that Beethoven probably was in a hurry.

It's an interesting challenge to your feeling for the sonata style if you eventually come to believe that the piece simply is too short, or that "something's missing." At a first impression all seems well, and we have a brief but effective essay in Beethoven's mature, middle-period style; but the better you get to know it, the more the proportions may start to sound out of balance. The result isn't so much bad as it is unsatisfying or incomplete. You may not hear it that way, and heaven knows nothing is wrong with that, but do listen a few times to see if you don't agree that this is the one overture that never quite lives up to the promise of its introduction. Indeed, it doesn't even try, and for that reason it might make the best impression—not as an independent concert piece but in the context of its original theatrical setting.

King Stephen, composed at the same time in 1811, is another matter entirely. It may not be "great" Beethoven, but it certainly gets the job done. The opening brass fanfare returns ingeniously as the accompaniment to the second subject, while formally the piece is as effective as it is simple: a slow introduction followed by two jolly themes in quicker tempo, a very slightly modified repeat of that whole operation, and a coda based on the same material. Best of all, the tunes are obstinately memorable, especially the positively adorable clucking woodwind theme of the introduction, which you get to hear three times—at the beginning, the middle, and the end. We will look a bit more closely at the occasions for which Beethoven wrote both this overture and *The Ruins of Athens* in our discussion of the theatrical music, but you don't need to know anything about the backstory to enjoy the music perfectly well as it stands.

The last of Beethoven's theatrical overtures in our list was his very first: *The Creatures of Prometheus*, the introduction to an allegorical ballet whose scenario is lost, so, happily, we don't have to bother with it. Short, peppy, brilliantly scored, and immaculately crafted formally, the piece originally ran directly into the ballet's first number, an exciting storm scene, but with a concert ending it has been popular virtually since its premiere in 1801. This is Beethoven's second-shortest overture, after *The Ruins of Athens*, but unlike that work, *Prometheus* makes a perfect, self-contained concert opener, although one in the style of the contemporaneous First Symphony.

The introduction is brief but noble, with a memorable main theme on the horns and woodwind supported by a warm cushion of strings. This sets up a dazzling Allegro. The first subject isn't a tune, but a texture—a perpetual-motion motive on the violins supported by a strongly rhythmic accompaniment. Like the first movement of the *Eroica* Symphony, the music is in 3/4 time, with strong accents on the weaker second or third beats to provide that characteristic "Beethoven bounce" without letting the music lapse into obvious waltz tempo. Because the first subject is in perpetual motion, the piece has no need for distinct "motion music" to make the transition to the second subject, an ethereal flute duet. The (perpetual) motion music returns one last time, leading to a spiky closing theme in sharply accented descending scales parceled out among the various instrumental sections.

Beethoven arranges the transition to the recapitulation very cleverly: it starts in a minor key and includes bits of the just-heard closing theme, so pretends to be a development section until the music returns effortlessly to the home key of C major as if to say, "What are you worrying about? We've been home all along." From there on, the recapitulation is regular, leading to a racy coda that brings the overture to a close in a mood of unvarnished high spirits. In short, the piece is a gem and an ideal introduction to Beethoven's early style as a composer for the theater.

Concert Overtures

Coriolan
Leonore Overture no. 2
Leonore Overture no. 3
Namensfeier (Name-Day Celebrations)
The Consecration of the House (*Die Weihe des Hauses*)

Beethoven invented the concert overture as an independent musical composition, even though operatic or dramatic overtures had long been featured in concert programs individually. By "concert overture," we mean a piece of music in one movement, almost invariably in sonata form, which may or may not have been inspired by some external subject, and which is not intended primarily for use in the theater. Three of the five works under consideration here fall into this category, whereas two—the *Leonore* Overtures nos. 2 and 3—were intended as operatic preludes before Beethoven realized how inappropriate they were for that purpose. They became concert overtures by default and have remained so ever since. If you believe that this general definition sounds vague, you have a good argument. The concert overtures are a highly varied bunch.

Nonetheless, all of them have certain features in common, most obviously the presence of extensive development sections akin to those in symphonic first movements (though they still avoid exposition repeats). They are thus longer and larger than the theatrical overtures considered in the previous chapter, sometimes significantly so. The two big *Leonore* overtures, for example, play from between twelve and fifteen minutes each. This not only makes them far lengthier than a typical operatic prelude of the period, but they also are longer than the opening movements of most of the symphonies. Beethoven's first "official" concert overture, *Coriolan*, deserves a closer look on account of these and other special qualities that herald the arrival of a new symphonic medium of expression, one that would come to dominate much of the remaining nineteenth century.

Some Beethoven scholars, relying on biographical evidence, question whether *Coriolan* was intended as a concert overture from the very start. Inspired by German playwright H. J. von Collin's tragedy of 1802 (and not Shakespeare's *Coriolanus*, which tells the same basic story), the piece was performed once as a prelude to the play in 1807, but only after it already had been presented in concert. It is also curious that, unlike his other theatrical projects, Beethoven had the piece ready well in advance of that single staging, and he wrote no other music for the occasion—no songs, choruses, entr'actes, or scene-change music. It was a stand-alone effort, which makes it far more likely that Beethoven intended the piece primarily for concert presentation. Leaving aside issues of logistics, then, let us see what the music itself can tell us.

The plot of the tragedy is simple and straightforward: A successful general and military hero, Coriolanus runs for the office of Roman consul. He is defeated through political treachery, and his outrage leads him to be exiled. In order to take revenge, he makes an alliance with Rome's enemies to conquer the city, but his mother and wife successfully convince him to abandon his destructive plans. This understandably irritates his current allies, the Volscians, who were looking forward to sacking Rome; and, depending on which version of the story we're talking about, Coriolanus either commits suicide (von Collin) or is assassinated by the Volscians (Shakespeare).

The first thing to note about the overture is that *Coriolan*'s scoring uses Beethoven's standard symphonic forces for the period, with only two horns, not the larger ensemble typical of his music for the theater. This is also the only Beethoven overture (or concerto, or symphony, for that matter) that ends quietly, another point that favors concert performance. After all, the whole point of a theatrical overture is to signal to the audience that the show is about to start, and nothing does this better than a powerful, crowd-silencing conclusion. *Coriolan*'s quiet ending provides the crucial bit of evidence revealing Beethoven's intentions more generally, and it establishes the work as an especially clear example of what "program," or descriptive, music in his view can and cannot do.

For example, the play is a tragedy that ends in the death of its protagonist; and if the dark, mournful, fragmented ending of the overture doesn't signal "death," then nothing does. Before getting to that point, the story concerns two main characters, or groups of characters: Coriolanus himself, full of rage and bent on vengeance; and the women in his life, who plead for calm and attempt to restore peace. Sonata structures are especially strong in their ability to depict human characters defined by the emotional expression that their themes and motives convey. Accordingly, the *Coriolan* Overture takes shape as a battle between two opposing moods, embodied in its first and second subjects. Beethoven signals the ultimate failure of the forces of reconciliation by the simple expedient of playing the relevant music in Coriolanus's minor key, and this leads inevitably to the tragic closing pages.

The overture begins in a fury, with no introduction. As I mentioned previously, the music depicting Coriolanus is basically one giant temper tantrum in Beethoven's personal key of C minor. It consists of numerous abrupt, energetic, and oft-repeated rhythmic gestures, crescendos, and "bounce" patterns that occasionally assemble themselves into the outline of a tune. The major-key second subject is just the opposite, smoothly lyrical and long breathed. A lengthy closing paragraph introduces yet more of what we might call "Coriolanus music," even more vicious than before, representing a logical reaction to the preceding lyrical section.

This passes directly into the development, which is entirely athematic—it's basically one long, nervous twitch. Imagine Coriolanus pacing back and forth, wringing his hands, and muttering to himself. A decision seemingly reached, the music returns briefly to the opening bars and then to a varied recapitulation that is even more hysterical than previously. Indeed, each time the Coriolanus music returns, it sounds even more unhinged. The consoling second subject, on the other hand, remains unflappably calm until the coda, where it suddenly turns to the minor and, musically speaking, "gives up" the effort. One last return of the opening gesture, now growing progressively weaker, signals Coriolanus's ultimate demise.

The above description may or may not conform to Beethoven's own specific intention; it merely is one possibility consistent with both the course of the music and the action of von Collin's play. The point I want to stress, however, is that despite the many possible responses to the overture's expressive content, it unquestionably tells a story, from start to finish. This is the last factor separating *Coriolan* from the theatrical overtures. It is so complete a narrative all by itself that it renders the play unnecessary. As I also suggested in the previous chapter, this was exactly the quality that led Beethoven to jettison the *Leonore* Overtures nos. 2 and 3 in favor of the more clearly preludial *Leonore* no. 1 and *Fidelio*; and it is, first and foremost, what makes them—although Beethoven didn't realize it initially—concert overtures.

Take a moment now and consider how Beethoven manages to capture the essence of the play in purely musical terms. He doesn't bother with details of the plot, which music, in any case, mostly is powerless to express; nor does he bring in minor characters, who would necessitate time-consuming diversions or digressions. The focus remains entirely on the expression of contrasting feelings and their resultant interaction, not on literal "painting in tones." This distinction, in fact, would become Beethoven's own description of his approach to illustrative music in connection with the Sixth (*Pastoral*) Symphony (although, as you will see, not as it's popularly represented).

However, one particular controversy that Beethoven's overture potentially clarifies offers an opportunity for some very entertaining speculation.

If you recall, I mentioned that Shakespeare's *Coriolanus* ends differently (assassination) than von Collin's *Coriolan* (suicide). British writers especially, for some reason, have been at pains to insist that Beethoven's *real* inspiration must have been Shakespeare—first, because they're British and take a proprietary glee in trying to work Shakespeare into any conversation; and second, because von Collin's play is supposed to be trash and Shakespeare's a masterpiece. I believe that the music answers this question definitively: Beethoven follows von Collin. Why? Because the musical illustration of death by assassination would require the introduction of additional thematic material—representing the Volscians, or some other kind of dramatic intervention—whereas in Beethoven's overture, Coriolanus's music very graphically self-destructs. In other words, it's clearly a suicide.

The two other concert overtures that feature narrative or programmatic elements are, of course, the *Leonore* Overtures nos. 2 and 3, and it's fascinating to compare them, because they are based on exactly the same thematic material but handle it so differently. Both begin with slow introductions based on Florestan's aria "In des Lebens Frühlingstagen," a slightly different version of which appeared as the central episode in the slightly later *Leonore* Overture no. 1. This tune also will become the second subject in the main allegro sections of nos. 2 and 3, after the presentation of almost identical first subjects. The principal differences in the introductions and expositions, aside from numerous small details in scoring, dynamics, and texture, stem from the fact that Beethoven takes much more time over the initial presentation of his material in *Leonore* no. 2, trimming and compressing as much as possible in no. 3.

As the music progresses, the reason for Beethoven's strategy becomes evident. *Leonore* no. 2 has a very dramatic and extensive development section, full of unexpected incidents and clearly suggestive of exciting "stuff happening." It culminates in two offstage trumpet calls, the moment in the opera that announces the arrival of the king's minister and hence the defeat of the evil Pizarro's plot to kill Florestan (Leonore, aka Fidelio, had been holding Pizarro at gunpoint and threatening to kill him anyway). In the opera, at this occurrence the scene changes as Leonore, Florestan, and all of the prisoners emerge from their dungeon cells into the bright sunlight to celebrate their newfound freedom, and Pizarro gets his comeuppance. This is exactly what happens in *Leonore* no. 2—Beethoven cuts straight to a triumphant coda and concludes in appropriately festive fashion. In other words, the shape of the overture tracks the plot of the opera very closely. In formal terms, it consists of an introduction, exposition, development, and coda. Note the absence of a recapitulation.

Beethoven noted it, too.

Accordingly, the *Leonore* Overture no. 3 contains the recapitulation of the first and second subjects missing from no. 2, but this new emphasis on formal symmetry has a paradoxical effect. Instead of making the new overture less dramatic than its predecessor, it became far more so, and it pays to try to understand the reasons why. In the first place, all of those nips and tucks that Beethoven performed on the introduction and exposition of no. 3 to make them shorter result in a much higher level of tension, because the entire scheme of musical incident happens more quickly than before, with less repetition and a higher degree of contrast. It's also worth noting in this connection that both overtures play for almost exactly the same amount of time, even though no. 3 reveals a more extended articulation of its overall form.

Similarly, while the lengthy development section of no. 2 is very colorful and inventive, it is also episodic—that is, it consists of multiple events spread out over a relatively broad area. The far shorter development of no. 3, on the other hand, consists of a single pattern—a loud crash with rushing strings followed by a fragment from the introduction—repeated several times, from which the music attempts (in vain) to escape with a more lyrical bit of melody. It is similar in this respect to the development in *Coriolan*—a musical representation of being "stuck in a rut." It needs something momentous to get it moving once again. Suddenly, a minor-key version of the first subject cuts in and drives the music to a crisis, thrillingly interrupted by the two trumpet calls (a bit different from the ones in *Leonore* no. 2). In other words, instead of multiple incidents, this development section contains only a single supremely dramatic moment, but one whose special character and importance are heightened by its context and presentation.

After this central crisis, the recapitulation, introduced by a flute in duet with the bassoon—the happy reunion of Leonore and Florestan, perhaps—is highly compressed. It comes as a welcome contrast and relief. The music is now audibly "back on track," just in time to introduce the most exciting coda that Beethoven ever wrote, with its tornado of string scales and epic, dissonant climax right before the end. In retrospect, its power and energy also make everything that came before somehow more vivid and impressive. If *Leonore* no. 2 reveals music's ability to capture and pursue a literary narrative, then no. 3 shows what happens when that narrative is reshaped and reinterpreted as a purely musical process.

You might say that no. 2 *describes* the story depicted in *Fidelio*, whereas no. 3 *embodies* it. Both are inspired by its principal themes of selfless love, heroism, and freedom from oppression, and neither is necessarily better than the other. Indeed, it's probably more helpful not to think in a negative way of no. 3 as a revision of no. 2, in the sense of a correction, but rather as a new piece based on the same material but written entirely from scratch. It's impossible to deny, however, that *Leonore* no. 3 is universally regarded as one of Beethoven's very greatest (and most popular) works, whereas no. 2 remains a comparative rarity in concert. Taken on its own terms, it's still a terrific piece, and hopefully this brief discussion will allow you to approach it in the most receptive frame of mind.

Beethoven's last two concert overtures, *Namensfeier* and *The Consecration of the House*, aren't about anything at all in a literary sense. Like the sitcom *Seinfeld*, however, sometimes a show about "nothing" turns out to be quite something, at least as a source of entertainment. For some reason, in case you were wondering, *Namensfeier* is always called that, even in English-speaking countries, whereas *The Consecration of the House* is seldom referred to as *Die Weihe des Hauses* outside of Germany. It's a horrible title either way, to be honest, although we will see that, after a fashion, it is accurate.

Actually, the true name of *Namensfeier* (Name-Day Celebrations) is *Zur Namensfeier* (For the Name-Day Celebrations), referring to the feast of St. Francis of Assisi on October 4, which was the name day of Austrian Emperor Franz I. Although the overture was intended for that event in 1814, it wasn't ready in time, and Beethoven didn't finish it until 1815. He simply called it a "Grand Overture in C Major" intended for any suitable occasion requiring a good musical introduction. The piece still hasn't really caught on, probably because its title suggests something solemn and elevated in tone, whereas the actual music, once past the lovely introduction with its evocative horn theme, is coarsely humorous and energetic, even by Beethovenian standards.

The overture is also tricky for the orchestra. Cast in a lilting 6/8 meter (like the main body of the Seventh Symphony's first movement), the music is full of offbeat accents and syncopations; and once it gets going, it never lets up. One of its most important ideas occurs in the motion music between the first and second subjects. In the coda, this becomes an especially outrageous "Beethoven bounce" in the form of a sort of jolly, heavy-handed tarantella that chugs along for several pages of score. In short, *Namensfeier* contains about seven minutes of consistently entertaining music that does exactly what Beethoven intended: it puts the audience in a good mood for whatever program follows. It certainly deserves to be better known, although happily it enjoys numerous first-rate recordings. Indeed, it's one of those works that's almost impossible to get wrong.

The same can't be said of *The Consecration of the House* (TCH for short), an exhilarating major work that just about everyone agrees is one of the most formally curious things that Beethoven or anyone else ever composed. It consists of a march, a fanfare, a passage of excited anticipation followed by mysterious calm, a huge double fugue on two themes in what Beethoven regarded as "Handelian" style, and an equally huge coda—all integrated into a single continuous movement that somehow makes perfect sense in performance even though there's no special reason for any of it to take the shape that it does. Beethoven wrote the piece to inaugurate a new theater in Vienna at which a revised version of his music for *The Ruins of Athens* was being produced, so you might also call this piece "The Ruins of Athens" Overture no. 2, but the various *Leonore* overtures are confusing enough, so we won't go there.

TCH is an important work in Beethoven's output: it is the only orchestral piece, aside from the Ninth Symphony, that fully reflects the style of his last period. At this time, he became interested in the contrast (and conflict) between the sonata style and baroque, contrapuntal forms, specifically fugues. Now, a "fugue" simply is a piece in several parts (called "voices") in which the main theme, or "subject," is announced by each voice successively, as in a round. This, not surprisingly, is called the fugue's "exposition," whereas the bits between presentations of the subject are called "episodes." These two textures alternate, with the subject being treated in a variety of inventive ways—for example, closely overlapping, played backward, or upside down (inverted)—until the composer decides he's done all he wants to with it and brings the fugue to a theoretically impressive conclusion.

If sonata forms are dramatic, then fugues are strongly rhetorical—more like a discussion or an argument. They don't "go" anywhere; on the contrary, they stand their ground and build up a structure in a kind of musical architecture. You might say, then, that THC very appropriately celebrates the dedication of a new building by creating its equivalent in music. Beethoven had always written fugues, even orchestral ones such as the fugal episodes in the finale of the *Eroica* Symphony. However, in his late period he began to feature them extensively as part of a larger dialectic process, combining the opposing forces of drama and rhetoric in a new and highly effective expressive synthesis.

The works that show this process most clearly are the late piano sonatas and string quartets. Orchestral fugues present special problems because the large number of different instruments makes it virtually impossible to preserve the feeling of the music being written for a limited number of voices. The subject necessarily will jump around between instrumental groups of widely different timbres, and all kinds of accessory parts will be doing other things, such as providing accompaniments or banging out the rhythm. This makes the fugue in THC, as well as those in the Ninth Symphony, very special in Beethoven's compositional output, and it partly explains why this overture always has been considered something apart from his more typical orchestral writing. It really *is* different.

Aside from the big fugue at its center, the overture has all kinds of other distinctive and unusual features. For example, the scoring calls for trombones, used only during the opening processional march, and then for the sole purpose of echoing each phrase. This simple "call-and-response" technique greatly enhances the solemnity of the proceedings; but once the march has passed, the trombones rest for the remainder of the overture. The ensuing fanfare, for trumpets and timpani, punctuated by slashing chords from the rest of the orchestra, features incredibly virtuosic, difficult-to-balance, rapid runs in the bassoons, memorably described by writer Donald Francis Tovey as the sound of "hurrying feet." The next section is another march, this time a quick one with the theme rising and falling in a manner similar to the initial procession but much faster—perhaps a rush to the door, swiftly rising to a climax—followed by a deep and expectant calm.

Out of the stillness, a series of humorous queries tossed back and forth by the woodwinds and strings initiates a rapid accelerando as, all of a sudden, the orchestra "finds" the fugue themes, much as it will discover the famous "joy" melody in the finale of the Ninth Symphony, and we're off to the races in music of dazzling and inexhaustible energy. From here on, all Beethoven asks you to do is sit back and enjoy the ride. You may notice an especially arresting moment a couple of minutes in, where the music seems to get stuck on a stubbornly persistent harmonic plateau that leads to a temporary closing gesture in the wrong (minor) key.

The fugue actually ends with a grand, baroque-sounding cadence in slower tempo, featuring a trill in all of the violins, and the last two-plus minutes comprise a big coda in pure sonata style, full of harmonic twists and turns. Just as at the start of the fugue, Beethoven's writing gives the distinct impression of an active process of discovery; in this case, the goal is to find the only possible ending to this extraordinary work. Notice the cutoff to the timpani roll before the end of the very last chord, an effect that produces an extra feeling of finality. Both Tchaikovsky and Sibelius were very fond of halting their music's accumulated forward momentum in similar fashion.

The Consecration of the House brings to a fitting climax Beethoven's contribution to a medium in which we find the same formal variety, expressive adventurousness, and high level of inspiration that we will encounter in the larger concertos and symphonies. That makes them ideal "overtures" with which to begin your personal explorations of his music more generally. Their smaller size proved no barrier to his questing spirit, and all of the elements that make his personal style so innovative play a role here as well. They pack a lot of great music into a relatively small space. In other words, don't let the fact that you might not have a lot of time to spare prevent you from getting your Beethoven fix.

Interlude 1
Dance Music

Twelve Contredanses, WoO 14
Twelve Minuets, WoO 7
Twelve German Dances, WoO 8
Gratulations-Menuett, WoO 3
Musik zu einem Ritterballett (*Music for a Knight's Ballet*), WoO 1
The Creatures of Prometheus, ballet, op. 43

Discography

Dance Music (except Prometheus)
Swedish Chamber Orchestra/Thomas Dausgaard (spread around Complete Beethoven Orchestral Music series)
Academy of St. Martin-in-the-Fields/Neville Marriner (WoO 7, 8, and 14)
Tapiola Sinfonietta/John Storgards (includes Knight's Ballet)

Prometheus Ballet Music
Scottish Chamber Orchestra/Charles Mackerras
Orpheus Chamber Orchestra (no conductor)
Orchestra of the 18th Century/Franz Brüggen
Turku Philharmonic Orchestra/Leif Segerstam
Swedish Chamber Orchestra/Thomas Dausgaard
Staatskapelle Berlin/Günther Herbig (with Knight's Ballet)

All of Beethoven's dance music is early, with the exception of the *Gratulations-Menuett* (Congratulations Minuet) of 1822. Indeed, the *Knight's Ballet* of 1791 is the earliest piece of orchestral music by him that we have. Lasting about twelve minutes, and interestingly scored for an orchestra of strings, timpani, piccolo, pairs of clarinets, horns, and trumpets, but no oboes or bassoons, the piece contains eight tiny numbers: a march, German song, hunting song, a romance (touchingly scored exclusively for pizzicato strings), war song, drinking song, German dance, and a coda. Typically for Beethoven, even at this early date, the coda is one of the largest numbers in the piece.

As you might expect, the music won't win any awards for profundity, but it is charming, energetic, and tuneful. It also may be difficult to find—there aren't too many recordings and they tend to come and go in the catalog, so there's no need to make a special effort. However, I have pointed out a few in the discography above. If you find it coupled to something you want more, consider it a bonus.

All of the great Viennese composers wrote ballroom dance music. It was part of their "bread-and-butter" work, and most of it, being composed for specific occasions or onetime use, was considered disposable. Very little of the total survives. Dances for the public are mostly short—lasting one or two minutes in total—formally simple (usually ABA), rhythmically predictable to keep the dancers from tripping over themselves as they execute the prescribed steps, and usually written in sets of six or twelve. Some of Beethoven's, not included here, were composed for two violins and bass, which could be enlarged to orchestral proportions as the size of the room (and noise level) demanded. Those for full orchestra often make up for their limited formal resources by being very inventively scored.

Each piece in a larger set often has its own distinctive color. The use of the piccolo in addition to flutes in Beethoven's dances is almost standard. No. 10 of the Twelve Minuets adds an extra pair of muted horns to create echo effects. Percussion instruments, such as bass drum, cymbals, and triangle, appear in no. 10 of the Twelve German Dances, and that set contains a coda to round things off that not only brings back the bass drum, but throws in a posthorn solo (cornet) for good measure. We find a tambourine in no. 8 of the Twelve Contredanses, and no. 7

is the most famous of all: Beethoven's first use of the tune that would conclude the *Prometheus* ballet, feature in the *Eroica* Variations for piano solo, and turn up as the finale of the *Eroica* Symphony.

It's worth taking a moment to consider why this tune might have fascinated its composer to such a degree.

One of Beethoven's most noteworthy characteristics as a composer is his use of musical materials that can only be called "populist." This was a deliberate choice, one that undoubtedly was related to his revolutionary egalitarian and republican political sentiments. It cost him a tremendous amount of effort. His sketches reveal version after version of his most famous tunes, the process being not so much one of elaboration but of simplification—of finding the most essential, most natural, and most directly expressive final form of his ideas. The iconic example of this process must be the "joy" theme from the finale of the Ninth Symphony, a tune of such primal inevitability that it hardly sounds deliberately composed as much as borrowed intact from some deep well of our collective subconscious. The *Eroica* theme, as we'll call it, is a melody of similar type.

What makes these ideas so special isn't just the fact that they exist, but that Beethoven uses them to express his most powerful, even sublime and transcendental musical thoughts. They embody for him the grandeur and greatness of the ordinary, the mundane, and ultimately, the human. These are the qualities that made Beethoven everyman's composer and that give so much of his music its universal appeal, even to listeners otherwise uninterested in "the classics" as such. They allowed his art to be absorbed into the very fabric of Western culture (and beyond), so it's typical that one of the most telling examples of this phenomenon has its roots here, as no. 7 of the Twelve Contredanses.

As to the dance types themselves, the minuet (however it's spelled) was the dance of the eighteenth-century aristocracy. In its ballroom version, it's a stately piece—so the men's dress swords and women's massive skirts don't get tangled—with three beats to the measure, in 3/4 time. None of the beats is stressed very firmly, again to provide for a smooth, elegant, gliding motion through the steps.

A German dance, by contrast, has the same meter and moderate tempo as the minuet but is more rhythmic, with a hard accent on the first beat and often a clear secondary stress on the latter two. Many barrel organ and carousel tunes, such as the famous "Ach! Du lieber Augustin," are German dances, and they are closely related to the Austrian Ländler and other precursors of the waltz. In fact, Beethoven calls the final German dance in the *Knight's Ballet* "Walzer."

Finally, a contredanse is a quick piece "in two"; that is, 2/4 time, often with a folklike or open-air feeling about it. Often spelled "contradance" in English, its character is even more clearly defined by its alternative English name: country dance. Sets of these pieces in succession became organized into the eighteenth- and nineteenth-century quadrille, and as a kind of group dance featuring multiple couples following an alternating succession of step patterns, it is related to the American square dance.

The *Gratulations-Menuett* is Beethoven's only other significant, stand-alone dance piece. It was offered as a good-natured tribute for the name day of Karl Hensler, the theater impresario who commissioned Beethoven to revise his *Ruins of Athens* incidental music for rededication of the Josephstadt Theater in Vienna. The same event produced *The Consecration of the House* Overture. This is a symphonic minuet, longer and more highly developed than a true work meant for actual dancing, and some scholars suggest that it might have been intended originally for the planned Tenth Symphony, although for that purpose the music, which lasts only about four minutes, sounds distinctly unambitious.

Finally, we have Beethoven's only full-length ballet: *The Creatures of Prometheus*. As mentioned in the previous chapter in considering its popular overture, we don't really know what the individual dances described. We can be sure that the plot is very allegorical and very enlightened and leave it at that. Dating from 1801, the same time as the First Symphony, the music of the complete work always has had its detractors, but of its kind it's undoubtedly a masterpiece. Just consider the fact that no one cares about any other ballet by any other composer of the classical period but this one. Also, at the premiere the work was only a modest success because its individual numbers were considered "too learned," which is always a good thing in the ballet world if you want to listen to the music alone.

Interlude I

The complete piece, as it stands, contains sixteen dances (not counting the overture) and plays for between sixty and seventy minutes, on average. That makes it Beethoven's largest purely orchestral work in any form. Aside from the joyous overture and the finale featuring the famous *Eroica* theme, you also get a terrific thunderstorm, a gorgeous adagio for harp and solo cello that sounds almost like proto-Tchaikovsky (no. 5), a delicious pastorale (no. 10), and a wonderfully evocative number (no. 14) featuring solo Bassett horn—a rare member of the clarinet family with a range slightly lower than the standard model. Neither harp nor Bassett horn is used in any other major work by Beethoven. In short, the ballet is chock-full of beautiful, rewarding music, and he obviously lavished much care on its composition.

As you can see, many recordings are available on both modern and period instruments. The outstanding versions probably are those by Charles Mackerras and the Scottish Chamber Orchestra, and the conductorless Orpheus Chamber Orchestra, but if you want a delightfully anachronistic, uber-romantic view, try the Segerstam on Naxos. The music accepts this treatment surprisingly well, and like almost everything by Beethoven, you really can't fail by "going big." Taken as a whole his dance music isn't all that voluminous and, in strictly musical terms, perhaps not that important (whatever that means), but it's unquestionably worth sampling. Certainly, *Prometheus* is essential.

Part 3

Concertos

Discography (listed by soloist(s)/conductor)

Piano Concertos nos. 1–5 (complete cycles)
Mitsuko Uchida/Kurt Sanderling
Claudio Arrau/Alceo Galliera
Yefim Bronfman/David Zinman
Leon Fleisher/George Szell
Vladimir Ashkenazy/Georg Solti
Rudolf Serkin/Rafael Kubelik

Piano Concerto no. 1 in C Major
Martha Argerich/Giuseppe Sinopoli
Boris Berezovsky/Thomas Dausgaard
Arturo Benedetti Michelangeli/Carlo Maria Giulini
Sviatoslav Richter/Charles Munch

Concertos: Orchestration (in addition to strings and timpani)

Work	flutes	oboes	clarinets	bassoons	horns	trumpets	solo(s)
Piano Concerto no. 1	1	2	2	2	2	2	piano
Piano Concerto no. 2*	1	2		2	2		piano
Piano Concerto no. 3	2	2	2	2	2	2	piano
Piano Concerto no. 4	1	2	2	2	2	2	piano
Piano Concerto no. 5	2	2	2	2	2	2	piano
Triple Concerto	1	2	2	2	2	2	piano, violin, cello
Choral Fantasy**	2	2	2	2	2	2	piano
Violin Concerto	1	2	2	2	2	2	violin
Romance no. 1*	1	2		2	2		violin
Romance no. 2*	1	2		2	2		violin

*no timpani
**plus six solo voices and chorus

Part 3: Concertos

Piano Concerto no. 2 in B-flat Major
Martha Argerich/Giuseppe Sinopoli
Boris Berezovsky/Thomas Dausgaard
Murray Perahia/Bernard Haitink

Piano Concerto no. 3 in C Minor
Arthur Rubinstein/Erich Leinsdorf
Boris Berezovsky/Thomas Dausgaard
Rudolf Serkin/Leonard Bernstein
Emil Gilels/George Szell (Orfeo)
Arturo Benedetti Michelangeli/Carlo Maria Giulini
Annie Fischer/Ferenc Fricsay
Sviatoslav Richter/Kurt Sanderling

Piano Concerto no. 4 in G Major
Wilhelm Kempff/Ferdinand Leitner
Murray Perahia/Bernard Haitink
Wilhelm Backhaus/Hans Schmidt-Isserstedt
Ivan Moravec/Martin Turovsky
Friedrich Gulda/Horst Stein
Boris Berezovsky/Thomas Dausgaard
Claudio Arrau/Colin Davis
Stephen Kovacevich/Colin Davis

Piano Concerto no. 5 in E-flat Major (*Emperor*)
Nelson Freire/Riccardo Chailly
Rudolf Serkin/Leonard Bernstein
Rudolf Kempff/Ferdinand Leitner
Robert Casadesus/Dimitri Mitropoulos
Arthur Rubinstein/Erich Leinsdorf
Rudolf Firkušný/William Steinberg
Claudio Arrau/Colin Davis

Violin Concerto in D Major
David Oistrakh/André Cluytens
Jascha Heifetz/Charles Munch
Itzhak Perlman/Carlo Maria Giulini
Christian Tetzlaff/David Zinman
Wolfgang Schneiderhan/Eugen Jochum
Arthur Grumiaux/Colin Davis
Nathan Milstein/William Steinberg

Romances nos. 1 and 2 for Violin and Orchestra
Pinchas Zuckerman/Daniel Barenboim (with Piano Concerto op. 61a)

Piano Concerto in D Major, op. 61a
Peter Serkin/Seiji Ozawa
Boris Berezovsky/Thomas Dausgaard
Jenő Jandó/Béla Drahos (with Triple Concerto)
Daniel Barenboim (piano and conductor; with Violin Romances)

Triple Concerto for piano, violin, and cello in C Major
Sviatoslav Richter/David Oistrakh/Mstislav Rostropovich/Herbert von Karajan
Yefim Bronfman/Gil Shaham/Truls Mørk/David Zinman (with Septet)
Géza Anda/Wolfgang Schneiderhan/Pierre Fournier/Ferenc Fricsay
Jenő Jandó/Dong-Suk Kang/Maria Kliegel/Béla Drahos (with Piano Concerto op. 61a)
Beaux Arts Trio/Kurt Masur (with Choral Fantasy)
Walter Hendl/John Corigliano/Leonard Rose/Bruno Walter

Choral Fantasy
Rudolf Serkin/Leonard Bernstein
Yefim Bronfman/David Zinman
Menahem Pressler/Kurt Masur (with Triple Concerto)

Just about every violin or piano soloist, major or minor, who has ever made recordings has taken a shot at one or most of Beethoven's concertos for their instrument. Most entered the repertoire within a few decades of the time that they were written, and they have remained there ever since. Even relative rarities, such as the Triple Concerto and the piano version of the Violin Concerto (listed as op. 61a), or the oddball Choral Fantasy, enjoy multiple recordings and are now easy to find in excellent performances. The above discography offers plenty of options, with first-rate versions listed in no special order of preference.

However, when it comes to the less familiar works, I have made an effort to choose recordings with convenient couplings and have listed them accordingly. It's handy to be able to get, say, the Triple Concerto and the Choral Fantasy on a single disc, although the latter also often comes coupled with one of the contemporary piano concertos. I haven't listed multiple recordings of the two violin romances, short works that just about everyone who plays them does well, and often appear alongside versions of the Violin Concerto. You'll probably get them repeatedly in the normal course of collecting, whether or not you feel that you need them. The same observation holds true for the Choral Fantasy—it always appears attached to something else, so you can either try to get one of the listed versions (as coupled) or simply take it as it comes along the way.

With respect to the five piano concertos, you have the option to get a complete set or individual works. All of the sets listed are worth having, and they have no weak performances. For decades the reference edition has been Fleisher/Szell, and it still makes an excellent place to start. The First and Second Piano Concertos very often come coupled on a single disc, and if you choose that option, Martha Argerich is very hard to beat. I include the performances by Arturo Benedetti Michelangeli of the First and Third Concertos because they offer two fine examples of this exceptional but idiosyncratic artist, who made relatively few recordings. If you already know the music, or come to know it well, give Michelangeli a shot for a refreshing change of pace.

Among the other classic versions, Claudio Arrau or Rudolf Serkin are always worth considering, and Mitsuko Uchida's complete cycle with Kurt Sanderling is staking a strong claim to be considered the modern reference edition, but I wouldn't want to be without Arthur Rubinstein in the Third Concerto, or Ivan Moravec and Stephen Kovacevich in the Fourth. No great recordings exist of any of these concertos on period instruments, but you can find excellent performances using modern pianos with orchestras trained to play in "historically informed" style. These include the versions listed by Bonfman/Zinman and Berezovsky/Dausgaard.

It has become common in recent years to see Beethoven (and Mozart) piano concerto performances and recordings conducted by the pianist from the keyboard. Some of these may be good if only because most orchestras today are trained to such a high level that they can play the music by themselves. In addition, some pianists, such as Vladimir Ashkenazy, also are good conductors, although not usually at the same time. The fact remains that the best performances always feature a conductor, if only because leading from the keyboard tends to force players to think about the need to wave at the orchestra rather than focus exclusively on their own part. On the other hand, ensembles left on their own can play very accurately, but just as often rigidly or mechanically. Also, collaboration between a great soloist and a great conductor offers telling proof of the old adage that "two heads are better than one." You will note that except for the Barenboim recording of Op. 61a, all of the recommended recordings in the discography feature separate conductors.

Regarding the Violin Concerto, you can't go wrong with any of the versions listed. Of the "golden age" violinists, Jascha Heifetz, Nathan Milstein, David Oistrakh, and Arthur Grumiaux remain the standard bearers, and their recordings haven't dated at all. The Perlman/Giulini recording did a lot to erase that soloist's reputation as a somewhat shallow virtuoso and elevate him to the status of supreme "artiste." As with the piano concertos, the Tetzlaff/Zinman recording has the advantages of a "historically informed" approach, with none of the disadvantages, but I retain a special fondness for the Schneiderhan/Jochum, a sort of apotheosis of the German school of violin playing, with its lean, finely focused tone and restrained use of vibrato. Scheiderhan also uses a violin adaptation of Beethoven's own crazy first movement cadenza from the concerto's piano version, with its daring timpani solo.

Finally, let me add a word on the Triple Concerto, one of Beethoven's least popular works for reasons we will discuss shortly. The reference recording for decades has been the Richter/Oistrakh/Rostropovich/Karajan, mainly for the quality of the soloists, but a lot can be said for hearing it played by a regularly constituted piano trio, such as the Beaux Arts, or for letting the historically informed approach, such as Zinman's, present the piece in a somewhat different, more vigorous light than we're used to (but, intriguingly, not more so than Bruno Walter's mono version from 1949).

General Introduction to Concerto Forms

Despite having only three movements, most concertos are as long, or longer, than contemporary symphonies. The reason is because they tend to have extremely large first movements. If you've ever wondered why this is the case, you've come to the right place. We will answer this question in detail. First movement sonata form in classical concertos is one of the most subtle and sophisticated inventions in all of music. Learning about it provides a direct entry into the mind of the composer and goes straight to the heart of how Beethoven's concertos operate and, therefore, what they express. Happily, the formal strategies that we will explore in this chapter require nothing in the way of advanced technical knowledge because the main issues are, fundamentally, matters of logic and good sense.

The kind of classical concerto form that gets all of the attention in textbooks and most written commentary was invented by Mozart; eventually it was adopted by Beethoven in just five works: the Triple Concerto, the Violin Concerto, and the Third, Fourth, and Fifth Piano Concertos. That's it. Later, it was revived by Brahms in his four concertos, but the vast majority of similar works by composers from the classical period onward simply ignored Mozart's version of classical form, either because it was too much trouble to bother with, or because they had no clue that it existed. Nor did they need it to write perfectly delightful concertos that were very successful in their time and remain so today.

"Form," then, to be honest, is merely one compositional aspect that goes into the making of a successful concerto, and not necessarily the most significant. I would say that two other elements are equally if not more important—far more so than in symphonies or overtures—and relate specifically to the presence of a featured solo instrument throughout the entire piece. The first of these is the tunes, which govern the expressive content and have to sound splendid when played by both the orchestra and the soloist. The second is *virtuosity*, the technical flash and dazzle, as well as the expressive intensity, which lets the soloist stand out against the much larger ensemble, creates excitement, holds the audience spellbound, and garners applause at the work's conclusion.

It's important to understand in this connection that "virtuosity" means much more than playing fast and loud, or executing daredevil tricks. It includes complete control over the instrument: sustaining shades of volume at all dynamic levels; the ability to generate a fine, singing (*cantabile*) tone; beauty of touch on the keyboard and sureness of intonation on the violin; and the ability to execute a perfect trill—the rapid oscillation between two notes that concludes so many solo passages and cadenzas. These are all qualities that the virtuoso must possess, and Beethoven's concertos demand them just as they demand skill in the more pyrotechnical aspects of performance. The Violin Concerto is a challenge in terms of sheer endurance alone.

Indeed, the quality of virtuosity as a means of grabbing your attention and "cheating the clock" is such a powerful factor that many concertos can sustain their length quite well despite being pretty much dysfunctional, formally speaking. I mean, if the piece is a showstopper, who cares if the tunes are repeated endlessly rather than developing in a meaningful way?

To give you an example of what I'm talking about, consider for a moment one of the most iconic examples of formal pointlessness: the famous first movement of Tchaikovsky's Piano Concerto no. 1. It starts with a grand introduction. A heroic summons on the horns leads to bold, thrilling piano chords covering the whole span of the keyboard, and this is mere accompaniment to one of the most gorgeous tunes ever to flow from a composer's pen. The whole process goes on for several minutes and is developed to the point where you might well think that you're listening to a completely independent piece. It has absolutely nothing to do with the main body of the first movement and fulfills no structural purpose relative to what follows. But when it comes to showing off the soloist and blowing away the audience, it totally delivers the goods and has deservedly made the concerto a popular favorite. You'd have to be crazy to consider the work in any way unsuccessful because the first movement introduction does nothing meaningful other than exist for its own sake.

Moreover, the remainder of the first movement (once we finally get to it) employs a perfectly regular example of sonata form. Tchaikovsky treats it as a convenient external framework or vessel to contain the tunes and allow for periodic displays of solo virtuosity. This is quite different from letting the form define the terms of the solo's participation with the orchestra in an overarching symbiosis, one that requires both actors to work together toward shared expressive goals. Mozart, and later Beethoven, achieved just this sort of collaboration between solo and orchestra in their concerto first movements, and it is why they often were so long. The process, as you will see, takes time. In considering how they did it, we'll first examine the problem in historical perspective, and then later explore a practical example, Beethoven's Third Piano Concerto, in detail as we examine the individual works.

The modern concerto evolved in the seventeenth century out of the baroque opera aria, in particular the type employing what became known as "ritornello form." This is much simpler than it sounds. A ritornello is, as the word implies, something that returns—a refrain or repeated phrase. Arias employing this form begin with a tune, or ritornello, which alternates with the singer's solo episodes. These can feature new ideas or stick closely to the opening melody, in any proportion the composer chooses and the text suggests. The bits of the ritornello between the episodes usually are fragmentary, varied, or appear in different keys, until the whole thing comes back in the home key at the end. That's the entire deal. It's really not all that different from your average "verse and refrain" type of song, or another musical form that we encounter very frequently in Beethoven and elsewhere: the rondo. Substitute an instrument for the voice, and you have a baroque concerto.

An archetypical movement in ritornello form will have three solo episodes punctuated by four complete or partial statements of the ritornello, including the ones at the beginning and the end, but this can be expanded as necessary. The orchestra does not normally stop during the solos, but rather accompanies lightly and interjects brief comments here and there. In the last solo, however, the orchestra often will pause completely for the *cadenza*—that is, an improvised section that permits soloists to display their virtuosity and (theoretical) good taste by making up a lengthy, dazzling passage on the spot based on the themes heard so far. Shorter cadenzas might appear anywhere else, too, depending on the course of the music and on how much of the solo part the composer bothered to write down.

From this basic description, it should be evident that the circular shape of the typical ritornello aria is the very antithesis of the dramatic, goal-directed, evolving sort of movement that characterizes the classical sonata style. The challenge for Mozart and Beethoven lay in finding a way to combine the two methods effectively. It wasn't enough simply to dump ritornello form in favor of the sonata, if only because the alternation between solo and *tutti* (full orchestral) sections in the earlier style makes so much practical sense and, let's face it, will happen anyway. I mean, whenever a tune is repeated more than once, you basically have a ritornello, and the whole point of a concerto is to give the soloist numerous, specific opportunities to show off. Hence the need for well-defined episodes. So, what's a genius sonata-form composer to do?

The key, as it turns out, concerns the initial presentation of the work's principal ideas. Because a movement in sonata form represents a kind of musical drama, you can well imagine that the way in which the main characters (themes) are introduced is critical. We already have seen that Beethoven's overtures and symphonies employ special versions of sonata form, so it stands to reason that the concertos will, too. In this case, the composer has to deal with the fact that the dramatic action will be expressed in tandem by the orchestra and a soloist who, in addition to carrying forward the expressive message of the work overall, has to negotiate an entirely separate cooperative relationship with the larger and more powerful ensemble so that both can display what they do best without either ever sounding inhibited or unnaturally restrained.

The orchestra's opening ritornello thus has a double purpose in the sonata style: first, to present the main characters in the drama; and, second, to introduce the soloist. Both tasks are equally important, and the secret to success lies in the difference between a ritornello theme in, say, a baroque concerto or a rondo, and a "subject" in a sonata exposition. The former is just what the words imply: a single tune. It may be long or short, but it unquestionably constitutes one idea. A "subject," on the other hand, may contain any number of melodies or motives, bound only by their location in the same key area.

These can be arranged to create suspense and give the listener the feeling of hearing an *introduction* to an important moment, such as the first entry of the soloist. For example, giving some of the themes a marchlike character suggests the effect of a purposeful procession and helps to create a sense of expectation. Beethoven's enthusiastic use of trumpets and timpani in all of his major concerted works, except the Piano Concerto no. 2, highlights this aspect and would have qualified them as "grand military concertos" in their day. Even that Second Piano Concerto opens with an orchestral fanfare in march rhythm.

However, a composer can do more things to make his exposition as effective as possible, and these relate specifically to the workings of sonata form. The entry of the solo, so long delayed, is bound to be a major event, but what should the soloist actually play? Remember that in classical symphonies—and all of Beethoven's up to the Ninth—the exposition usually is repeated. His overtures omit the repeat, but the concertos use it as an additional mechanism to highlight the critical formal role of the soloist. Mozart already had realized that if he avoided moving decisively to a new key for the exposition's second subject, he could save this maneuver for the repeat and make it the soloist's job.

This was a very subtle but, formally speaking, crucial discovery. It gives the composer additional wiggle room, not just with respect to the key scheme of the movement, but more critically in determining which themes and motives go where. It doesn't mean that logic flies out the window—for instance, that the first theme we hear will be placed out in left field somewhere in the exposition repeat—but it does allow for changes in emphasis with respect to the initial material, its function, and relative importance. The idea isn't to be unnecessarily complicated but, rather, to keep the ongoing dialogue between the soloist and the orchestra always fresh and surprising so that your attention as a listener remains consistently engaged.

In all of his mature concertos, Beethoven seized on this concept with relish. The initial exposition serves as an introduction, building anticipation; although the ideas that will become the second subject may give evidence of wanting to move to new keys, hinting at what's to come, the drama only begins when the soloist enters and repeats the exposition with the orchestra. This procedure gives all of the initial material its true, dynamic form by organizing the themes in their definitive order and in their proper keys. If you hear concerto first movements described as having a "double exposition," this is what the term means: an expository ritornello for orchestra alone, followed by the repeat with the soloist, structured according to the tonal dictates of the sonata style.

It follows, then, that the exposition repeat in a classical concerto often will be longer and more extensively developed than the initial, ritornello-style introduction. It can include new ideas, often introduced by the soloist, and feature plenty of motion music, usually in the form of expressive and virtuosic solo passages omitted initially because of the need to prevent the music from "going" anywhere too soon. With the presence of the solo made absolutely necessary, indeed essential to the symphonic argument, both the orchestra and the soloist now are free to develop the characters defined by the concerto's themes, working together collaboratively. Accordingly, once the solo enters, don't expect to hear a uniformly strict alternation with the orchestra, as may happen in the older, baroque ritornello form. There will be moments of stark opposition, naturally, often to mark the end of major sections, but also every degree of dialogue and interaction between solo, the orchestra, and all of its various constituents.

Finally, two significant additional consequences to this situation are worth noting. First, the recapitulation will need to take into account any differences between the first-time exposition (the ritornello) and the repeat. It will not be strictly identical to either, so it offers even more opportunities for expressive nuance. Second, when the recapitulation culminates in a *cadenza*, whether improvised or not, it gives the soloist a spotlight similar to what the orchestra enjoyed at the start of the concerto—a moment to take the stage all by itself. If you add up all of these factors, it should be clear why classical concerto first movements are so long. They really do have a lot to accomplish. Here, for example, are average first movement timings for all of the Beethoven concertos:

Piano Concerto no. 1: 16'30"
Piano Concerto no. 2: 13'
Piano Concerto no. 3: 15'30"
Piano Concerto no. 4: 18'
Piano Concerto no. 5: 20'
Violin Concerto: 23'
Triple Concerto: 17'

You may well wonder how much of the above process you will recognize when you listen in real time. The answer depends on how well you know the music. The more familiar it is, the more details come to light. Initially, if you simply feel a sense of anticipation leading up to the entry of the soloist, and enjoy the ensuing recasting between solo and orchestra of material that you have just heard played by the orchestra alone, then you will have understood all you need to as regards form. My experience is that the entry of the solo after the ritornello is so immediately vivid and arresting that any idea of it being part of an "exposition repeat" serving a crucial structural purpose flies completely out the window and consequently notions of form, as such, become irrelevant. This probably is as it should be. Concertos don't exist to display their form; they exist to show off the soloist and create a compelling dialogue with the orchestra. The formal element, however interesting or sophisticated it may be, merely offers support.

I have provided this lengthy explanation because knowing why the music is organized in a certain way allows for listening with greater concentration—not just to what the music expresses but to how it communicates so powerfully and effectively. Also, Beethoven's concertos, those for piano especially, offer the opportunity to hear a fascinating process in motion. We need to remember that he began his career as a barnstorming virtuoso. He premiered the first four piano concertos himself, and they were composed for his own use. As he matured, however, Beethoven the virtuoso gave way to Beethoven the composer. From about 1802 onward, he knew that his days as a star attraction at the keyboard were numbered due to his growing deafness. By the time he composed his Fifth Piano Concerto in 1809, he could no longer perform his own music; and as you will see, this had implications for his handling of first movement concerto form.

As for the concerto's remaining parts, it is a rule of classical period works that the most complex movement, formally speaking, invariably is the first. After that, the music becomes progressively more relaxed. Both the slow movement and finale (usually a rondo) will be shorter and less formally challenging; and now that the soloist has been effectively introduced into the proceedings, no rules or special considerations govern how the solo and orchestra interact. It's all smooth sailing, as the next two chapters hope to show.

Piano Concertos

Beethoven's five completed piano concertos confirmed their featured solo's replacement of the harpsichord as the keyboard instrument of choice for the new century. They represent, without question, *piano* music in both sound and technique, from the pen of a composer who was one of the great virtuosos of his age. In their day they were considered the most modern, forward-thinking, and daring works of their kind. Their progressiveness, however, extended beyond questions of mere keyboard technique to encompass every parameter of their formal elaboration and musical substance. Like the symphonies, they reveal a systematic path of progress from the earliest works to the latest, despite the fact that all of them were composed over a span of little more than a decade and a half. It pays, then, to describe them in chronological order of composition, although obviously you can listen to them in any way that you choose.

Piano Concerto No. 2

Owing its numbering to its later date of publication, Beethoven's Second Piano Concerto is really his first. He famously described it as "not one of my best." This doesn't mean that the music is bad. Beethoven still thought it worth having printed, assigned a value to it, and so should we. The music is delightful and, besides that, so helpful in allowing us to hear the distance that Beethoven traveled from this journeyman work of circa 1795 to the *Emperor* Concerto of 1809. Actually, part of an even earlier piece, dating from 1784, survives. It needs major reconstruction in order to render it performable, so we won't consider it here.

After spending an entire chapter discussing the joys of Beethoven's first movement concerto form, it may amuse you to learn that as far as this piece is concerned, he might as well not have heard anything about it. The first movement's two expositions are just that: two separate expositions. They have very little to do with each other, in theme or structure. The concerto opens with a descending fanfare in vigorous rhythms: dum, dadum, dadum, dadum. This dominates the opening and conclusion of the orchestral ritornello, which has a more lyrical interlude in the middle touching on several foreign keys—so the first exposition has a distinct, ABA shape and comes to a firm close before the piano enters with completely new material. The initial fanfare turns up in the solo's motion music between first and second subjects, and briefly at the end of this second exposition, but otherwise the soloist mostly minds his own business.

With so much material to work with, you can well imagine that Beethoven is spoiled for choice over what to develop later on, never mind how to assemble a logical sequence of events in the recapitulation. These details you will enjoy discovering for yourself. Beethoven composed an excellent cadenza for this movement much later (around 1809). It seems to take note of the loose structure of the music to this point, because it opens with a fugato based on the opening fanfare and acts almost as a second, more thorough development section. The contrast between the discursive character of the movement as a whole and the rigorous thematic workmanship of the cadenza makes for a nicely compact, focused introduction to the difference between Beethoven's youthful and mature styles.

The slow movements of Beethoven's concertos usually adopt some type of song form (ABA) or "sonata form without development" such as we heard in the theatrical overtures—but because the tempo is slow, the length of the movement is much longer. This means an ABAB shape, but the simplicity is deceptive for a couple of reasons. First, the larger structure conceals many opportunities to enlarge the form with new themes, encouraged by the slow speeds of both the motion music between A and B—aka the first and second subjects—and the central transition to the recapitulation. Second, the presence of the soloist permits a lot of variation and ornamentation of the melodic material, especially in the recapitulation. You will never find the music to be static or merely repetitious.

Especially in the concerto slow movements, then, we have little need to discuss details of form when the overriding impression will be of a lyrical dialogue between the soloist and the orchestra. Even in this early example, the slow movement reveals Beethoven as a mature artist capable of giving his music exceptional expressive depth. The opening hymn has an almost religious character, which is very typical of his movements in adagio tempo (or slower). This is a quality he probably got from Haydn, who often did something similar in the adagios of his symphonies. Mozart usually prefers quicker speeds to propel his inimitable, cantabile melodies. The orchestration of the hymn when it returns in the recapitulation, distributed between the solo and the orchestra, is absolutely heavenly.

Beethoven's concerto finales are all rondos, albeit with a strong sonata-form overlay. The standard rondo has five sections—ABACA—but Beethoven's sonata version usually has seven—ABACABA, not counting cadenzas or codas added besides. In this structure, A and B function as first and second subjects respectively, which explains why they return later to make up a formal recapitulation. The central C section takes the place of the development and often features a new episode in a minor tonality (if the home key of the movement is major). The present example is Beethoven's shortest and most schematic, with an infectious, spunky principal theme full of lively syncopated rhythms. This was the second finale that Beethoven wrote for the concerto, the first being the Rondo in B-flat Major, WoO6, which shows that he put the same kind of effort into this piece that he did for all of his largest and most serious compositions.

One additional element peculiar to Beethoven's concerto finales is worth noting. At the very end, the music often seems to lose energy dramatically, humorously, or poetically (or all three), providing a few moments of reflection before the exciting conclusion. Again, we first encounter this gambit here, but it will reappear in much more grown-up form later on. Altogether, despite some tentative spots in the first movement and the smallest orchestration of any Beethoven concerto—no clarinets, trumpets, or timpani—this music has genuine charm, plenty of showmanship for the soloist, and in its slow movement a decided foreshadowing of the great things to come.

Piano Concerto No. 1

This concerto represents a quantum leap over its predecessor in terms of expressive grandeur and formal sophistication. The use of trumpets and timpani has an amazing impact on the sound of the work as a whole. It's astonishing how small changes can transform a score. For example, Beethoven employed march rhythms even more obsessively in the ritornello of his previous concerto, but here he captures an even more martial effect, whether or not those rhythms are present. It reminds us that sheer sound, in the form of instrumental timbre, often has a meaning all its own, independent of the melodic or harmonic context in which it appears.

In addition, all of the basics of Beethoven's mature, first movement concerto form are now in place, except that the ritornello's second subject perhaps goes too far in placing itself in a decidedly different key—or rather several of them. Nevertheless, in this passage we see the first example of a kind of melody that would serve Beethoven especially well in the Fourth and Fifth Piano Concertos and in the Violin Concerto. This is a tune that touches on, or modulates, in stages through several keys, never settling firmly in any of them. It gives the opening ritornello a wonderful splash of harmonic contrast and tension without compromising its essentially introductory quality. In his later concertos, Beethoven learned how to do this with complete assurance and tremendous subtlety. Here, not so much, but you get the point all the same.

Far more important to understanding this first movement, and indeed much of Beethoven's later work, is the fact that he seizes on the rhythmic form of the opening motive (long-short-short-short) and uses it as the principal constructive element of the entire movement. This technique forms the backbone of Beethoven's mature style, so much so that you can recognize entire movements from just looking at their proprietary rhythmic signatures. Sometimes the three short notes detach themselves and function independently, but their derivation from the opening theme is always clear. Pay attention to this readily audible guidepost. It allows you to relax and enjoy the interplay between solo and orchestra with complete ease and confidence.

The second movement, marked Largo and so even slower than the previous concerto's Adagio, starts with a theme that resembles the first few notes of the song "I Don't Know How to Love Him" from *Jesus Christ Superstar*. This is the sort of music that renders formal analysis pointless. What you hear is a seemingly endless stream of lyrical melody constantly exchanged and embroidered by both the piano and the orchestra. Beethoven gives the clarinet an extremely important additional solo role, for the first time in any of his orchestral works, and at a time when the instrument was still something of a novelty. Its use here was one more aspect of the concerto's modernity when it first appeared, and it remains for us now an outstanding example of Beethoven's melodic beauty.

If you're familiar with any of Haydn's rondos and other music in the "Hungarian" style, then you will find this finale to have a characteristic lilt, especially when it comes to that catchy central, minor-key episode. The main tune, as previously, is strongly syncopated and full of rhythmic energy, but as befits this concerto generally, everything happens on a larger and more expansive scale. Indeed, at close to forty minutes' playing time, this is a very substantial work by any standard. The finale's coda takes Beethoven's fondness for a reflective interlude before the end to new heights, offering a moment of mesmerizing, nostalgic stillness before the comically abrupt ending.

Piano Concerto No. 3

This is Beethoven's only concerto in a minor key, his personal one of C minor, in fact, which gives some idea of its outstanding qualities.

Because the music appears with this book on the accompanying website, I will provide a detailed outline of the entire work with additional commentary as necessary so that you can follow it section by section. If you already have a preferred performance and its movement timings are similar, you can still use this outline as a guide. As we've been discussing, sectional breaks in classical concertos usually are very clear, made even more so in this particular work by the alternation of minor and major tonalities for its various themes.

First Movement: Allegro con brio Track 2

Exposition 1 (Ritornello)

The most noteworthy element to notice in the ritornello is the fact that Beethoven presents what will become the official second subject in a sunny major key. He plays it twice, but then immediately contradicts it, as if to say, "Not yet, folks." The music returns to C minor, and the closing section contains a large number of ideas all designed to confirm the fact that the momentary contrast the second subject offered was illusory.

Exposition 2 (solo and orchestra)

With the soloist now fully engaged, Beethoven completely recomposes and expands the transitional motion music between the first and second subject, letting the solo take the lead. The closing section, on the other hand, now that the second subject is firmly established in its contrasting, major key, can be shorter and, with the piano leading the charge, flow effortlessly into the development section.

Development

Returning largely to minor keys, the development is brief, nervous, and consists almost entirely of reiterations of the first subject's characteristic dum-dadum-dadum rhythm (that is what makes it sound so nervous). The orchestra has the rhythm in the bass, while the piano comments. The oboe and bassoon have important, lamenting, secondary solos.

Recapitulation

The recapitulation of the first and second subject, which now features the piano and the solo in free dialogue, is compressed, which is why I have left out entirely the idea of motion music in the above outline. With all of the music now in the key of C (minor, then major), Beethoven has no need for extensive transitional material. The formal exposition comes to a close in C minor, and a big climax leads to the traditional pause on an expectant chord (if you're curious because you hear what sounds like something similar in just about every classical concerto, in technical terms this is called a "6/4 chord"). The cadenza now gives the solo a chance to strut its stuff. It has an important job to do: review and comment on some or all of the themes of the concerto thus far, while still hammering home the main key of C minor so that the orchestra can conclude the movement in emphatic fashion.

Second Movement: Largo Track 3
Exposition

As in the previous concerto, the slow movement is extremely slow indeed. It opens with a piano solo playing a sort of chorale, immediately repeated by the orchestra. The mood is one of rapt stillness, so when the motion music kicks in, the tempo really does seem to pick up, like a sleeper gradually awakening from a deep dream. The piano once again introduces the second subject, having not participated in the motion music at all.

Development

The development is what they call in the music biz "episodic"—that is, based on entirely new material, giving the whole movement a kind of glorified ABA shape (if you consider A to be the full exposition). It consists mainly of a "moonlit" dialogue between flute and bassoon, accompanied by the piano playing rippling, liquid arpeggios (broken chords). Orchestral wind players wait eagerly for the opportunity to play this music, with good reason, and you can evaluate the soloist's artistic judgment and egomania quotient by his or her willingness to let the woodwinds take the spotlight.

Recapitulation

Whereas the exposition featured the main themes played by the solo and orchestra in sequence, now they offer them together, delicately embroidered and embellished. The very last chord, surprisingly, is strong and not soft, Beethoven once again breaking the music's spell and telling his listeners to wake up—this time to be ready for the finale, which accordingly works very well when played immediately, without a pause. In concert, this often is accompanied by lots of coughing, rustling of programs, stretching noises, and other signs of twitching and fidgeting, all signs of how well this exquisite Largo did its job.

Third Movement: Rondo: Allegro Track 4

This Rondo, although outwardly typical in shape, has several unique features resulting from Beethoven's especially clear amalgamation of sonata and rondo forms. The first of these is the central episode, which begins with an important clarinet solo but then turns into a sort of development section introduced by a fugato for orchestra on the Rondo's principal A theme. When this works its way back, finally, to the opening tune, the feeling is not merely one of "return" but of "recapitulation." It's an impossible distinction to describe adequately in words, the difference being purely musical, but I'm sure you'll notice it when listening.

The second special feature arrives in the form of an especially extensive, scampering, comic coda, in quicker tempo and in a completely different rhythm from the main body of the movement. This not only proves enormously refreshing while simultaneously completing the rondo form, but it sets a seal on the music's joyful relief at being truly free of minor keys once and for all. The coda is so frisky, in fact, that it has no time for Beethoven's frequent recourse to a moment of stillness just before the enthusiastic ending. Let me remind you in this regard that these and any other suggestions as to the music's expressive or emotional qualities are purely personal. What it all means remains for you to decide, always keeping in mind that no point of view is right or wrong.

Piano Concerto No. 4

Something about this concerto is almost magical, a quality evident right at the start. Beethoven lets the piano announce the main theme, solo, gently, with the orchestra answering timidly on a distant harmony. The beauty of this opening is breathtaking, and you could write an entire treatise on the way pianists have agonized over how to handle these initial bars. Should they be played simply and directly, strictly in time, or expressively, with small hesitations and accelerations? Should the dynamics be level, or subject to minute gradations? Does the pianist have a beautiful touch to begin with? Few clear answers emerge, but the point to keep in mind is that the concerto contains many such magical moments, and what makes them so mysterious and affecting is that all of them happen softly. The piece offers a clinic in the art of conquest by stealth.

Consider the first theme. It's based on a repeated rhythmic figure that happens to be exactly the same as the four-note "motto" of Beethoven's Fifth, and he will use it in this movement almost as obsessively, but the effect of gentle persuasion here couldn't be more different. The tune rises quickly to a climax—a brief outburst of motion music—before subsiding into a haunting march, largely for woodwinds accompanied by the strings, that modulates through several keys before ultimately reaffirming the tonic G major and tossing out a couple more brief motives to bring the ritornello, or first exposition, to a close. So far, so good, and just as the textbooks provide.

However, the second exposition, introducing the piano, has other ideas. You would think that the material of the movement's first and second subjects already has been defined clearly, but you would be wrong. In fact, the true second subject hasn't been heard at all. After a good bit of new material in the form of motion music from the piano, an entirely new theme appears in the orchestral violins, immediately taken up by the solo. The march only returns later, after plenty of discussion, to round off an entire paragraph that makes the second subject the longest and most diverse part of the exposition.

The introduction of new material turns out to be prophetic, because the development is almost entirely episodic—that is, only loosely based on previously heard material. In a very real sense, the dynamic of the first movement consists of repeated efforts to break away from the irresistible, magnetic attraction of the two main themes by trying out alternatives. It is a plan that comes to naught when the recapitulation begins loudly and emphatically, with the solo piano reasserting its dominance. It's the most physical moment in the entire movement. However, as I said at the start, all of this happens subtly, never with violence. The music has ample power, and Beethoven ensures that you feel it operating, but mostly behind the scenes. In keeping with this proposition, the scoring of the first movement omits the trumpets and timpani, which will make their surprise entrance only in the finale.

The magic continues into the Andante con moto (walking pace, with motion) second movement. Less than five minutes long in most performances, this is one of the most extraordinary creations in all of music. Scored only for piano and strings, it is a true dialogue—as in *spoken* dialogue. Hearing it is like watching a conversation through a pane of glass. You can see it taking place and read the expressions on the faces of the participants, but you can't make out the exact words, so the subject remains a mystery. The strings play forcefully (at first) in jagged rhythms, entirely in stern octaves, without harmony until the very end. The piano, on the other hand, answers with a soft chorale, all harmony in full, solemn chords. The two go back and forth, occasionally interrupting, but otherwise avoiding any simultaneous cooperation until the very last chord. That's it. All you have to do is follow the progress of the conversation and use your imagination.

This remarkable music has excited a huge amount of commentary over the years, usually centered on the question of what it all "means." The most popularly cited explanation came in the mid-nineteenth century from Beethoven's biographer and inventor of sonata-form terminology, A. B. Marx. He described the movement in mythological terms as representing Orpheus calming the Furies (Tovey replaced this last with "wild beasts" and attributed the whole thing to Liszt). This is charming, of course, but it ignores the fact that these Furies (or beasts) aren't especially ferocious (or bestial), and that the pianist (or Orpheus) becomes more agitated as the movement proceeds, not calmer. Oh, and the ending isn't exactly a happy one. Small details, right? Just about the only mythological reference to the music might be the dark final chord, which could very well be described as "Stygian."

Beethoven directs that the concluding Rondo proceed without a break, yet another example of him counteracting the effect of his deepest and most self-evidently profound music with a brisk splash of cold water, given additional impact by the addition of trumpets and drums. This movement builds on the more developmental aspects of the Third Concerto's finale and has the following shape: ABACBA-coda with cadenza. You may notice that we're missing an A, but this is illusory because the second episode, C, is a development of A, so Beethoven sees no need to repeat it again. The lead-back to A, whenever it occurs, is also very elaborate, so that you're never quite sure when the main theme will appear until it finally does. It's all good, clean fun, nowhere more so than when we realize that Beethoven gets the actual rondo business over with quickly so that he can devote nearly half of the movement to "the coda that just won't quit." It's that special Fourth Concerto magic again, in this case with more than a little sleight of hand.

Piano Concerto No. 5 (*Emperor*)

The title *Emperor* did not originate with Beethoven but, rather, with his English publisher. Appropriate or not, this is without question a grand, majestic work. At about forty minutes it is Beethoven's longest piano concerto, and his most popular, no doubt because of the opening—a thrilling alternation of crashing chords for full orchestra alternating with virtuoso piano riffs. It is the complete opposite of the opening of the Fourth Piano Concerto, although it obeys the same basic principle: let the piano lead off, and then proceed with the customary ritornello.

This raises an interesting aesthetic question. It's indisputable that having the soloist sit there, doing nothing for the entire initial exposition, looks strange; and, as music (including Beethoven's) became longer breathed and more virtuosic—in other words, more "romantic"—the long initial ritornello came to seem unnecessary. Beethoven must have agreed, given the way he begins his Fourth and Fifth Piano Concertos. Later composers, starting with Mendelssohn, often let the soloist start immediately, as a full participant, and not incidentally avoiding the problem of having to structure a disproportionately long first movement.

On the other hand, eliminating the ritornello also negates the opportunity to take advantage of one of the movement's most potentially dramatic moments: the entries (especially the first one) of the soloist. You can hear Beethoven exploit this very artfully in the first movement of the *Emperor* Concerto. After the ritornello, the piano appears with a quiet, rising chromatic scale. It becomes an instantly identifiable solo fingerprint, and that's exactly how Beethoven uses it, both for entrances and exits. It creates a curious feeling of tension and anticipation all by itself, and it would have counted for nothing had it not been preceded by the first exposition for orchestra alone.

As it turns out, the form of this first movement is unusually clear and spacious, adding to the music's feeling of "bigness." Both the first and second subjects as initially presented, along with several ancillary ideas, turn out to have the same functions in the solo's exposition. The second subject is yet another of those unforgettable, harmonically rich tunes that Beethoven uses to create contrast without having to commit himself to changing key, although, of course, he can when he wants to. Each time that it appears, this tune seems to take on a different expressive identity, from triumphant to almost cosmically mysterious, especially as it appears in the passage that Beethoven substitutes for the traditional cadenza (more on that in a moment).

In the Fourth Piano Concerto, we saw that the development section was largely episodic. This one is just the opposite. It's based almost entirely on the first subject, which undergoes a huge number of transformations shared by the piano and the orchestra across a vast terrain of musical acreage. The recapitulation, when it finally arrives, includes the entire introduction as well, a most unusual feature, but we learn at least one reason for it when, at the start of the coda, the orchestra pauses for the cadenza. There isn't one. Beethoven writes a note to the soloist (in Italian): "Don't make a cadenza, but proceed instead with the following," before writing out a brief solo passage that begins imposingly, then continues with that hypnotic, timeless version of the second subject.

Commentators have suggested many reasons for this innovation. Beethoven's deafness meant that this was the only piano concerto he never premiered personally, and it could be that he didn't trust the cadenza to anyone else. Also, the two presentations of the introduction already have offered the pianist plenty of opportunity for the sort of virtuoso display usually reserved for a cadenza, so Beethoven may have felt no need for more of the same. Finally, even without a cadenza, at an average playing time of twenty minutes, this is Beethoven's longest piano concerto first movement and one of his most tightly argued. Why risk messing that up, and trying the listener's patience, with yet more development of what we've already heard numerous times? Whatever the reason, out went the cadenza, and with that concerto history was made. Virtually every later composer followed suit.

The tranquil slow movement (Adagio un poco mosso—Slow but moving a bit) is of utmost simplicity. It has the form ABAA, with A being played first by muted strings, then in an ornamental variation by the piano, then the woodwinds by way of conclusion. B is a solo for piano that provides contrast. The return to A, begun on the horns, is delayed by a series of piano trills, rising higher and higher. That's all there is to it, except that the beauty of the themes speaks for itself. The movement never ends. It comes to rest on a sustained note over which the piano quietly hints at the theme of the concluding Rondo, which bursts out surprisingly, loudly, and with great gusto.

Beethoven organizes this finale as a sort of rondo-equivalent to the first movement. Its form, ABACABA, looks perfectly traditional, except that like the first movement, C is a substantial development section based entirely on A—the first subject. You also may notice that the flashy runs on the piano introducing B have their equivalent in the first movement's chromatic scales. Everything about this movement seems designed to recall the concerto's opening Allegro without needing to quote from it. You get a strong feeling that this music belongs to no other work. The coda features an important solo for timpani, as the music slowly winds down, coming to a complete stop, before the piano leads the orchestra in the rush to the close.

The *Emperor* Concerto is one of the iconic works of Beethoven's "middle period" and his last concerto for any instrument. We know that he planned a sixth piano concerto, but he never completed it. With deafness closing in on him, and instrumental virtuosity becoming a goal unto itself, he had little reason to write more concertos unless someone had the taste, intelligence, and foresight to ask him for one and the wherewithal to pay for it. Most budding virtuosi, in any case, were expected to write their own, proprietary music in order to display their talents, and Beethoven had little patience for them. It isn't astonishing, then, that despite all that he had contributed to the medium, he saw no reason to offer more.

Concerto and Romances for Violin

It's impossible to overstate the greatness of Beethoven's Violin Concerto. Cynical though it may appear, the reason is because it sounds more like Beethoven than it does a typical violin concerto. This doesn't mean that the writing is not idiomatic for the instrument—that it is—but rather that the forms Beethoven employed ensure that the twin personalities of violin and orchestra work together in pursuit of a higher musical purpose than mere display of the soloist's technical facility. In Beethoven's day, violin virtuosos came a dime a dozen, and all of them wrote concertos for their own use. The most important composer for the medium after Beethoven was Louis Spohr, who wrote around eighteen violin concertos between 1803 and 1844, plus other works for violin and orchestra. All of them have been recorded. No one cares; and Spohr was a very serious artist with (just ask him) an elevated standard of taste.

Beethoven's single work enjoys the value of scarcity and benefits from the fact that it was written for someone else, Franz Clement, who was important enough to be worth composing for but not so big as to be able to push Beethoven around and dictate what he wanted. This is a crucial point, because we find many more bad violin concertos than bad piano concertos. The piano has the ability to make a full mass of harmony effortlessly and oppose the orchestra on a more or less equal footing as a matter of course. The violin, on the other hand, requires special pleading. It can only stand out from the much stronger orchestra either by reducing the accompaniment to nothing, or by ferociously fiddling away at reams of notes in a continuous display of virtuoso pyrotechnics. This gets old pretty quickly.

So, the bottom line is that violin concertos are exceptionally difficult to write, and the composers who churned them out by the dozen only managed to do it by taking an assembly-line approach to problems of texture, form, and balance. It is a measure of Beethoven's greatness that not only does his Violin Concerto solve all of these problems in wholly individual ways, but it is his largest concerto for any instrument. It plays for a good forty-five minutes in a typical performance, with the first movement alone lasting around twenty-three to twenty-five. Indeed, it is the longest purely instrumental movement that he ever wrote, period, and for that matter just about as large as anything by anyone else who came later.

The reason for the concerto's great size, however, has nothing to do with grandiosity or complexity, but it simply results from the length and breadth of its melodies, their abundance, and their unhurried presentation. In other words, the form arises organically from the content, and all of it is designed to showcase the special lyrical, singing qualities of the violin without ever resorting to aimless noodling simply because stringed instruments can do that so easily. It contains virtuosity aplenty, but it's intelligent virtuosity, applied with purpose. Accordingly, the Violin Concerto isn't "exciting" in the traditional loud or fast sense—at least, not until the finale—but nonetheless it is full of incident, suspense, and both rhythmic and harmonic tension.

It should come as no surprise that so unusual a work was not a success at its premiere in 1806 at a benefit concert for its dedicatee, Franz Clement. Legend has it that the soloist had to fortify the audience with something more to its taste by performing a solo of his own composition, played entirely on a single string with the violin held upside down. Accounts differ as to whether he did this in the middle of the concerto or as an encore at the end, but either way you get the picture. Afterward, the concerto languished in relative obscurity until it was revived in London in 1844 by the young violin prodigy Joseph Joachim under conductor Felix Mendelssohn. The work quickly became Joachim's calling card, but the reality is that it didn't really catch on until later in the century, when violin virtuosos ceased performing their own, proprietary repertoire and instead focused on promoting the great music written for their instrument by the best composers. You have to wonder what took them so long to figure out that one.

The concerto's first movement is a miracle of musical architecture. Its broad outlines are incredibly easy and enjoyable to follow. Beethoven starts the work softly, with four solo taps from the timpani on the same note and in even rhythm. Some commentators mention that the taps number more than four on occasion, but the motive that Beethoven isolates and uses throughout the movement as an independent idea has only those first, four beats. Nothing can be simpler to remember, so keep it in mind. You will be amazed at how it keeps turning up, sometimes as accompaniment, sometimes as part of the melody. It is the glue that holds together the entire huge structure.

Beethoven presents his first and second subjects in the ritornello almost exactly as they will reappear in the solo exposition that follows, even making allowance for the violin's extra introductory material and additional embroidery over the melodies. Both subjects have two tunes each, and all but the last are stated initially by the woodwind section. This means that when the solo finally plays them, they automatically take on fresh colors; more important, they sound absolutely wonderful on the violin. Their appearance on the solo instrument represents a homecoming of sorts—one of those intangible qualities that you feel very distinctly nonetheless when you hear it. The same observation holds true for the character of the themes themselves: a wholly special, lyrical purity and innocence that have convinced many listeners to call the music "spiritual."

Between the first and second subjects comes motion music in the form of the only reliably loud gesture in the entire movement: a series of crashing chords for the full orchestra, with sharp, staccato jabs separating them. This idea will prove to be just as important as any, especially because its appearances always are unexpected and, therefore, so disruptive that Beethoven can indulge us in presenting the gentler, more lyrical ideas for long periods without running the risk of monotony. That's basically the entire deal: one motive; four unforgettably beautiful, luminous tunes; and a few bars of loud, strongly gestural motion music.

As I mentioned in chapter 1, the initial entry of the violin, rising in octaves like Venus emerging out of the waves on her seashell, constitutes the gentlest of all of Beethoven's "bounce" ideas. Also, like the later *Emperor* Concerto, the use of this characterful initial gesture goes a long way toward justifying the presence of the long opening ritornello and other orchestral passages that delay the arrival of the solo. By the end of the movement, we have come to await those violin octaves like the much-anticipated return of a long-lost friend.

Another aspect of Beethoven's treatment of the solo is worth noting. Because the violin tends to soar rhapsodically above the orchestral mass whenever they play together, it can present new ideas while the orchestra sticks with music that we've already heard. The development section, for example, probes a haunting, minor-key version of the first subject phrase by phrase, while the solo sings above the ensemble, sometimes embroidering the melody, sometimes evolving new ideas entirely. In other words, the development is both strictly bound by the opening theme and "episodic" at the same time, thanks to this concept of textural layering. You will hear something very similar in the slow movement.

In the coda, Beethoven has the orchestra pause for the traditional solo cadenza, and he never bothered to write down one himself—at least, not for the violin. This could have been disastrous, because the last thing we need after such a potent example of melodic grace and formal poise is some tactless fiddler hacking away for minutes on end to wow the audience with his virtuoso carnival routine. Happily, excellent cadenzas exist by Joachim and (the one most frequently used today) Fritz Kreisler. Beethoven did write down a cadenza for the work's piano concerto arrangement (op. 61a), a sometimes loony extravaganza that includes solo timpani having a field day with its four-note opening motive. This has been adapted for the violin, too, most notably by Wolfgang Schneiderhan in his recording under Eugen Jochum, which I mention in the discography.

Cadenzas also have been written in deliberately incompatible, modern styles, such as Alfred Schnittke's, recorded by Gidon Kremer. It is monumentally ugly, albeit deliberately so. If you don't know the Violin Concerto well, generally I recommend a performance that uses one of the standard cadenzas, or at least one not likely to prove too scary; but once you do know it, by all means feel free to check out the various alternatives as your mood dictates. Quite a lot of them exist, and the ones used normally are mentioned on the back of the CD tray, along with the other standard performance information and movement listings.

The second movement, Larghetto, offers an iconic lesson in artless simplicity that never becomes merely simplistic. The scoring, for clarinets, bassoons, horns, and strings, allows the solo to stand out in all registers and at all dynamic levels. Its form is completely free, and it is unique to this work. Here is the outline:

Theme A (muted violins)
    Variation 1: horns, clarinet, and violins, decorated by the solo
    Variation 2: bassoon, violas, and cellos, decorated by the solo
    Variation 3: forte in the full orchestra, no solo
        Solo reenters and makes a transition to:
Theme B: solo violin, running directly into:
    Variation 4: solo violin with pizzicato strings, brief transition back to:
Theme B: varied and ornamented by the solo, leading to:
Coda: Theme A, with a loud transition leading to a solo cadenza introducing the finale

It includes no major key changes or harmonic disruptions. Beethoven sustains a mood of utter tranquility, yet it's not true to say that nothing happens. As you can see, the movement, which plays for about nine or ten minutes, falls roughly into two halves. The first half includes the first three variations, and the role of the solo is purely decorative. It never gets the tune. After the loud third variation, however, the solo takes over with a new theme all its own, and then incorporates the opening melody into what becomes a continuous stream of song that persists all the way to the end. Once again, we hear Beethoven affirming the equality of the concerto's two main participants, solo and orchestra, but he does it with such a light touch that the process never draws attention to itself.

The Larghetto never comes to a complete close. After the solo cadenza at the end, Beethoven provides a few notes of transition and directs that the final Rondo proceed without a break. This movement also plays for about ten minutes, and as in the first movement, its length stems from the breadth of its melodies. The main Rondo theme, for example, almost always is played three times whenever it appears, twice by the solo (the second time up an octave, "delicately" as Beethoven asks), and then by the full orchestra. Naturally, this takes time, but the tune is so catchy that you never tire of hearing it—or at least that's what happens in a good performance. I once had the misfortune of hearing a major soloist (I'm not naming names) play the whole thing about a quarter tone sharp, which is the musical equivalent of fingernails scraping on a blackboard. It was excruciating.

Beethoven writes his Rondo in a galloping 6/8 time, which is "hunting" meter, quite literally. It's the rhythm used for the horn signals that accompanied aristocrats on their favorite outdoor hobby, and for the "B" episode we do get some genuine hunting music, horns and all. The form of this movement falls into Beethoven's standard rondo shape, with no unusual features: ABACABA, with the last statement of the main theme being a substantial coda preceded by one final cadenza for the soloist. As Beethoven nearly always does near the end, he relaxes the tempo and mood for a brief, reflective moment before the soloist pushes ahead, and the orchestra joins in for the joyful closing bars. Many feel that this extraordinary work remains the finest violin concerto ever written. That's saying a lot, but it's an opinion that really does deserve to be taken seriously.

Finally, we can't leave this discussion of the Violin Concerto without mentioning Beethoven's arrangement of the work as a piano concerto (op. 61a). This always has been controversial, denigrated, and largely ignored. Major pianists wouldn't go near it and, despite a few prior releases, this version languished until Peter Serkin recorded it under Seiji Ozawa for RCA Records at the start of the 1970s. Since then, many new recordings have followed as soloists search for underplayed repertoire by major composers on which to leverage their growing careers. This is Beethoven, after all.

The piano version unquestionably suffers in comparison with the original, which is so plainly devised with the special sound and technique of the violin in mind that Beethoven's decision to tamper with it seems incomprehensible. In particular, the violin's ability to sustain a lyrical melody endlessly and embroider a melodic line, as happens during the first half of the slow movement, for instance, has no keyboard equivalent. Also, consider the question of what the pianist is supposed to do with the left hand when all of the necessary accompaniments already have been allocated to the orchestra. Critics tend to treat Beethoven's solution to this problem with disdain, calling the revised piano part unidiomatic. It's a real problem in musical aesthetics.

It is true that the piano part is not especially difficult or virtuosic, but then neither is the original compared to the stuff that violin virtuosos routinely were churning out at the time. On the other hand, you do get the additional cadenzas that Beethoven composed expressly for the piano. As I mentioned, these have been reimagined for the violin by several soloists, but they often are dismissed with the same purist arguments, insisting that they sound better as originally designed for the keyboard. Also, every musical work has what you might call local and global qualities. These latter comprise all of the major formal elements that remain identical in both versions, and to the extent that they constitute the primary factors in the success of the work, they legitimize both equally.

Ultimately the matter remains one of personal choice, as so often is the case in these situations. Because the piano arrangement now is so readily available, listeners can try it out at leisure and make their own decisions as to whether one version sounds better than the other. Some people can't stand the sound of the solo violin; others love anything written for the piano on principle. The music remains magnificent either way, and there is no right or wrong.

Violin Romances in G Major and F Major

These two sweet, lyrical works for violin and small orchestra were composed in 1798 (no. 2) and 1802 (no. 1), respectively. They were published in reverse order; hence, their current numbering. We don't know exactly why Beethoven wrote them, or when they were performed in their original form. Concerts in the nineteenth century were grab-bag affairs, often consisting of miscellaneous movements from larger works, opera arias with famous singers, short pieces for solo and orchestra (or, in the absence of a large ensemble, piano)—in short, anything and everything that could pull in an audience. Countless brief, lovely, single movement works such as these have vanished from today's concert stages, and more's the pity.

Some enterprising soloists might consider putting together several such pieces to make up a full-length program, but the logistics are daunting. Few conductors would bother to learn them or agree to give them valuable rehearsal time, and audiences want to hear the "big" concertos. The situation is better on recordings, which is where works such as Beethoven's Violin Romances find their natural home as fillers to the Violin Concerto, or in collections of violin encores and other light music. As I mentioned in discussing the discography, you take them as they come.

Aside from being melodically seductive, the two romances offer perfect examples of the traditional rondo form: ABACA, with the C episode invariably using a contrasting minor key to add a touch of pathos. They also display the two different kinds of typical rondo themes. That in G major features the first type, which falls into two halves, both repeated, with the solo followed by the orchestra for each half: AABB. The main theme of the Romance in F Major features the solo playing the whole melody once through, then gives the orchestra a turn. Both types of movement derive, obviously, from the standard "verse and refrain" song form; and although the term wasn't coined until much later (by Mendelssohn), "songs without words" describes exactly what these pieces are.

Triple Concerto and Choral Fantasy

Every prolific composer, on occasion, will turn out works that defy categorization, are less popular, or seem to represent a lower level of accomplishment than the acclaimed masterpieces. This chapter discusses two of them. The fact that the music isn't easy to pigeonhole doesn't mean that it's bad. Deviations from the theoretical norm or preexisting expectations are bound to count against any work of art that requires time to make its points, especially in our present, impatient world, with its ever-shorter attention spans. On the other hand, some criticism is fair, and not everything by even the greatest composer needs to be hailed equally as a product of genius. Accordingly, the two works up for consideration here offer an ideal opportunity to draw your own conclusions and think critically while listening.

Triple Concerto

The Triple Concerto has earned a reputation for being Beethoven's dullest orchestral work, not entirely without reason. It is, in many respects, atypical of what he often leads us to expect from one of his major efforts. Even in his lightest and most happy pieces, we look forward to their irrepressible energy, their occasional rough edges, and their enlivening sense of struggle. His tranquility, too, has cosmic dimensions. Not here. In the Triple Concerto, everything is gracious, polite, and even—dreaded term—courtly. The aesthetic issues it grapples with are numerous and extremely complex, and it's an open (and very subjective) question as to whether Beethoven has solved all of them successfully—or even wanted to. Nevertheless, we will have a go and see what we can make of them.

First, let's understand just what this piece is: French. Specifically, it belongs to a category of concerto-like composition called the "sinfonia concertante." This is essentially a concerto with multiple soloists, and it was a preferred form of orchestral music in late eighteenth-century France, from whence it spread throughout Europe. Although today we consider the One True Path of music to pass through the Viennese school of Haydn, Mozart, and Beethoven almost exclusively, it's important to keep in mind that this is historically fallacious. In reality, many regional schools of composition existed, led by composers whose names still pop up now and then—if not in concert, then on recordings. Two of the most famous composers of concertante symphonies were England's J. C. Bach (the youngest son of the famous one) and Joseph Bologne, Chevalier de Saint-Georges, in France, who was an ace at fencing as well.

Haydn and Mozart wrote concertante symphonies as well. Haydn's, sometimes known as "Symphony no. 105," is a marvelous late work featuring solo violin, cello, oboe, and bassoon. Mozart wrote a couple of them, the most famous being the very great Sinfonia Concertante in E-flat Major for violin and viola, K. 364. Beethoven's Triple Concerto belongs to this tradition, but with a twist in the form of a piano. Most concertante symphonies require two or more melody instruments, which sets up a pretty straightforward balance of forces between the soloists and the orchestra. Toss in a piano, though, and the composer has to deal not just with questions of balance and texture regarding the solos and the orchestra, but also among the very unequal soloists themselves, as well as between the orchestra and piano independently.

Many insist that Beethoven never really resolves these problems satisfactorily. Having a full piano trio—that is, piano plus violin and cello—as a solo group begs the question of why you need an orchestra at all. Making matters more difficult for himself, Beethoven features the cello as the lead soloist despite the fact that the violin or the piano would have been more typical—and easily audible. Had Beethoven chosen that route, however, he effectively would have had to kiss the cello good-bye. As a result, the keyboard writing tends to be unusually light and mostly quite simple. It's certainly not a virtuoso part. This was a smart thing

Triple Concerto and Choral Fantasy

at the time, because it was written to be played by Beethoven's aristocratic pupil and patron, Archduke Rudolf, who was a good but not great pianist. But it certainly ducked the purely musical issue of doing justice in a concerto setting to the most potentially effective solo instrument.

On the other hand, if you're a form maven, like me, the Triple Concerto is an absolutely fascinating and very rewarding listen. The piece it resembles most is the Fourth Piano Concerto, in the structure of its opening movement as well as the very short and distinctive Largo that follows. Cynics will say that Beethoven took the lessons he learned in writing the Triple Concerto and then "got it right" in his next piano concerto, but I'm inclined to be more charitable and say that similar ideas can be turned to different but equally legitimate purposes.

Specifically, the first movement ritornello features two themes that seem destined to become the traditional first and second subjects. They follow one another without much motion music between them; but as in the Fourth Piano Concerto, the solo exposition repeat that follows contains a huge amount of additional material, with the previously advertised "second subject" only coming in toward the very end. In fact, this exposition has five distinct themes, only three of which occur in the ritornello. How Beethoven gets them all organized and sorted out in the course of ongoing exchanges between the orchestra and the three soloists is a beautiful and wondrous thing to hear.

Another charge leveled at the Triple Concerto is that because it has three soloists plus the orchestra, Beethoven has to play every important idea or passage four times, but this isn't really true. The violin and cello, in particular, have a tendency to pair up against the piano, thus reducing the need for repetition, while the keyboard does a lot of what keyboards always do: accompany everyone else. Multiple soloists also provide a wide range of instrumental color, preventing the remaining repetition from becoming monotonous. Finally, because this piece has no solo cadenzas, Beethoven finds room in the outer movements for two of his most imaginative "codas that just won't quit," and it's great fun to hear everyone throw caution to the wind and cut loose in the closing pages.

Indeed, given the fact that the slow movement only lasts about five minutes and flows directly into the finale, the Triple Concerto contains as much, or more, quick music as any other Beethoven concerto. The finale, a zesty Polonaise full of infectious rhythms, is the largest of all of Beethoven's concluding concerto movements. In short, the work as a whole looks exciting enough on paper, and yet it still has a reputation for dullness. After a lot of listening and pondering the matter, I can think of two basic reasons for this, one easy to describe, and the other easy to hear but rather more difficult to explain in words. I'll try anyway.

The first problem, one that tends to vanish on closer acquaintance, is the fact that the main themes in the first movement—all five of them—sound similar. They are all marches in moderate tempo, incorporating at one point or another a "dum dadum dadum" rhythm. It's hard to keep them straight, and their similarities initially blur the music's formal outlines while increasing the feeling of repetitiveness. It is impossible that Beethoven wasn't fully aware of this. He clearly chose relatively bland melodic material to emphasize the larger shapes he wanted to build out of it. In other words, the first movement is like a large building constructed of single-colored brick: from a distance it looks monochrome, but when you get up close you notice subtle changes in shading as well as all kinds of attractive patterns and designs in the way the bricks were laid.

After the first movement, the Largo holds out a promise of greater melodic interest. Its principal themes are gorgeous, but the movement functions as little more than an introduction to the finale. You hear the tunes once, and that's it. Happily, the principal theme of the Rondo alla Polacca is a doozy, especially in this context, but it's still the first really catchy theme we've heard in more than twenty minutes. So, if distinctive melody matters most, the Triple Concerto probably is not for you.

The above analogy to the soloists and orchestra as "brick layers" also speaks to the other main reason for the work's questionable reputation. Laying bricks isn't exciting. What I mean by this is that Beethoven's music, as we already have seen, usually generates tremendous forward momentum, even when (as in the Violin Concerto) he's not whipping up a storm. We always have a feeling of linear progress toward a goal. The Triple Concerto doesn't lack this quality; in fact, its goals are extremely clearly targeted. It just never seems to express any urgency to get to them because we're always being asked, moment by moment, to listen to multiple textural layers—to the bricks being laid. The music's vertical busyness, with the soloists and orchestra often doing several things at once, tends to break our perception of horizontal movement.

Once again, this is not an issue that Beethoven did not thoroughly understand. He obviously took great pains to give us sufficient time to let us hear exactly where the music wants to go, step by step, and he wanted us to enjoy the experience of getting there. The problem is that this measured approach can very easily sound didactic, and even more damagingly, cautious—something that Beethoven's music almost never is. In this respect, a lot depends on the soloists, who must ensure that their predominantly polite and euphonious dialogue never turns timid or precious. Also, there's a difference between savoring a moment and wallowing in it. The challenges the music poses in terms of taste and technique are thus quite different from what we usually expect in a concerto, never mind one of Beethoven's.

I want to emphasize, finally, that most of these difficulties primarily concern the first movement, because it's the most formally sophisticated. The Largo presents no special problems, and the finale is a typical Beethoven Rondo in ABACABA form, except that A is unusually expansive because of the number of participants involved; and as already mentioned, the final return of the main theme develops into an absolutely sensational coda featuring the Polonaise tune in a deliriously speeded-up variation. By all means, then, do give the Triple Concerto a shot, and if it doesn't strike your fancy at first, put it aside for a while and then come back to it periodically. I'm willing to bet you'll come around to liking it in the end.

Choral Fantasy

At first, you might think that this oddball piece has nothing in common with the Triple Concerto, but in fact it does: the highly individual treatment of the solo piano. The differences, however, are telling. Whereas in the concerto Beethoven felt the need to rein in the piano out of respect for his other soloists, here he puts the keyboard squarely in the spotlight, giving it the job of master of ceremonies. It warms up the audience with a solo set, introduces the other guests, and then participates fully in the final celebration.

Although it lasts only about twenty minutes in performance, the Choral Fantasy often sounds much longer than an equivalent concerto movement. This is because, absent the tonal framework of sonata form, you never know where the music is going. It lacks dramatic continuity as it progresses from one highly contrasted section to the next. Mind you, this isn't a defect. On the contrary, it's what makes the Fantasy fantastical—the unpredictable sequence of events, each of which is an enjoyable experience in itself.

In fact, the music doesn't lack structure. Much of it is in pretty strict variation form, but this island of order is merely the central episode nestled between the piano's opening solo and the choral conclusion. The overriding organizational principle is that of a steady crescendo from an introductory solo, to the full orchestra settling on the main theme, to the eventual recourse to actual words, with the music becoming ever more articulate as it passes through each major stage in its development. In this respect, it is very similar to what Beethoven does in the finale of the Ninth Symphony. Back in the old days of the long-playing vinyl record, before the compact disc made it possible to fit the entire Ninth onto a single disc, the Choral Fantasy made a logical "fourth side" coupling to performances of the symphony that required three LP sides, and thus two discs.

Beethoven was not happy with the poem. He wanted some words in praise of music and art and friendship, but not *those* words, which I provide below. If you think my flat, English prose translation following the German text looks tacky, nothing compares to the painfully alliterative original—never mind the many equally sappy English verse translations. German romantic poetry is notoriously soggy. No one has cared enough to establish the author of the verses with absolute certainty, and, perhaps not surprisingly, no one in Beethoven's day came forward to claim authorship. But if the music is great, it really doesn't matter what the shouting is about, does it? Anyway, Beethoven made do with what he had.

Schmeichelnd hold und lieblich klingen
unsres Lebens Harmonien,
und dem Schönheitssinn entschwingen
Blumen sich, die ewig blühn.
Fried und Freude gleiten freundlich
wie der Wellen Wechselspiel.
Was sich drängte rauh und feindlich,
ordnet sich zu Hochgefühl.

Wenn der Töne Zauber walten
und des Wortes Weihe spricht,
muss sich Herrliches gestalten,
Nacht und Stürme werden Licht.
Äuß›re Ruhe, inn›re Wonne
herrschen für den Glücklichen.
Doch der Künste Frühlingssonne
lässt aus Leiden Licht entstehn.

Großes, das ins Herz gedrungen,
blüht dann neu und schön empor.
Hat ein Geist sich aufgeschwungen,
hallt ihm stets ein Geisterchor.
Nehmt denn hin, ihr schönen Seelen,
froh die Gaben schöner Kunst
Wenn sich Lieb und Kraft vermählen,
lohnt den Menschen Göttergunst.

The harmonies of our life ring with graceful, charming, and lovely sounds; and the sense of beauty infuses the flowers that bloom eternally. Peace and joy proceed in friendship like the changing play of the waves. What was pressing roughly and hostilely now aligns in highest rapture.

If the magic of tones rules, and the consecrated words are spoken, a wonderful occurrence will turn night and storm into light. Outer calm and inner bliss will reign for the fortunate, for the spring sun of art transforms suffering into light.

The greatness that penetrates the heart blooms again in renewed beauty. A spirit flies upwards and a spirit-choir echoes in response. Take happily, you beautiful souls, the gifts of beautiful art. When love and strength unite, man earns the gods' reward.

Here is how the music proceeds:

1. Solo piano introduction leading to:

2. The so-called Finale. Lower strings softly make quizzical gestures answered by the piano. Sudden wind fanfares introduce the main theme, again played by the piano. This tune is plainly the prototype of the "Joy" theme in the finale of the Ninth Symphony.

Next come eight variations divided into two parts:

3. **Variations Part 1**: five simple or "strict" variations, closely following the outline of the theme. The piano, as master of ceremonies, introduces the members of the orchestra in the following order: (1) flute with piano accompaniment, (2) oboes with piano accompaniment, (3) clarinets with bassoon accompaniment, (4) solo string quartet, and then (5) full orchestra. This is followed by a "codetta," or "little coda" rounding off the section and leading on to:

4. **Variations Part 2**: three free variations in different tempos and keys developing various aspects of the theme, with the participation of the piano and the full orchestra. Don't expect to hear the full tune in these variations; when Beethoven's wants you to, you will.

Variation 6: Allegro molto, initially in vigorous exchanges between the piano and orchestra, but proceeding in several stages to:

Variation 7: Adagio ma non troppo, a clarinet duet interrupted by rhapsodic piano lines and bits of the tune on the lower strings, followed by a transitional passage to:

Variation 8: Marcia, assai vivace. This is exactly what the title says—a very vivacious march for the full ensemble, gradually calming down and leading back to the start of the finale, slightly abridged but colorfully embellished. This introduces:

5. Singing! The closing chorus takes the form of three further variations, the previous codetta, and the true coda in quicker tempo.

The choral "variations," when we get to them, are simple repetitions of the main theme scored for three solo women, three solo men, and then the full chorus, respectively. Each variation delivers a full verse of the text far more quickly than you'd be able to understand it, no matter the language. So don't worry about it. The only bit of the text that really matters, and always does come through clearly, is the last line, with the stress that Beethoven gives the words "love" ("Lieb") and "strength" ("Kraft"). He illustrates the word "strength," especially, with a big climax that comes around twice, and clearly inspired the even bigger choral shout on the words "vor Gott" ("before God") in the Ninth Symphony. Through all of this, the piano has been accompanying, commenting, and otherwise participating fully in the general celebration.

One puzzle that requires solving is Beethoven's designation of this main movement as a "finale." To what? You may well ask. It turns out that Beethoven planned the Choral Fantasy as the finale to an entire concert, specifically the endless and endlessly catastrophic benefit he organized for himself on December 22, 1808. The program included the premieres of the Fifth and Sixth Symphonies, the Fourth Piano Concerto, bits of the Mass in C major, the concert aria Ah! perfido, an improvised piano solo, and then, as the "finale," the Choral Fantasy. The hall was unheated, ticket sales were miserable, the soprano solo had stage fright, the orchestra broke down more than once, and the whole thing must have seemed interminable. Don't you wish you could have been there?

Interlude 2
Incidental Music

Egmont, overture and incidental music, op. 84
Die Ruinen von Athen (*The Ruins of Athens*), overture and incidental music, op. 113
König Stephan (*King Stephen*), overture and incidental music, op. 117
Triumphal March for *Tarpeja*, WoO 2a
Introduction to Act 2 of *Leonore*, WoO 2b
Funeral March for *Leonore Prohaska*, WoO 96

Discography

Vienna Philharmonic/George Szell (*Egmont*)
Berlin Philharmonic/Herbert von Karajan (*Egmont*)
Royal Philharmonic Orchestra/Thomas Beecham (*The Ruins of Athens*)
Berlin Philharmonic/Claudio Abbado (*Consecration of the House* aka *The Ruins of Athens*; *Leonore Prohaska*)
The Orchestra of St. Luke's/Dennis Russell Davies (*Egmont* and *The Ruins of Athens*)
Minnesota Orchestra/Stanislaw Skrowaczewski
Swedish Chamber Orchestra/Thomas Dausgaard (complete Beethoven Orchestral Music series)

This section offers a brief interlude about some (mostly) brief interludes. Beethoven devoted little time to writing for the theater. He started around 1810 with *Egmont*, and by 1815 he had had enough. There was only one significant exception: in 1822 he recast his music for *The Ruins of Athens* by writing a new overture (*The Consecration of the House*) and adding a couple of vocal numbers. The orchestral music for *Tarpeja* and *Leonore Prohaska* consists of tiny pieces lasting only a scant two or three minutes each, but if you happen to own Skroweczewski's fine collection of the complete overtures, you will get these numbers as well. The introduction to act 2 of *Leonore* (*Fidelio* before it became *Fidelio*) is also just a couple of minutes long and may be hard to find outside of complete recordings of the opera. Those, however, are much more commonly available than they used to be.

Beethoven's one major score for the theater is the incidental music to *Egmont*, and Szell's is the recording to own. You not only get the famous overture but four relatively substantial entr'actes (interludes between acts) and a very touching piece called "Clärchen's Death," which does exactly as the title suggests. She's Egmont's girlfriend, in case you were curious. The rest of the music, here and in the other large incidental scores, consists of songs and choruses, some well worth hearing, and melodramas—music underpinning spoken declamation. Take away the talking, and you can enjoy some of them as orchestral music as well. Karajan's recording also is worth considering because *Egmont* comes coupled to *Wellington's Victory* plus a rare selection of Beethoven's military marches (yes, he wrote a few).

Other than *Egmont*, the only other score that needs special mention is *The Ruins of Athens* (or, less familiarly in its revised version, *The Consecration of the House*). This not only contains the famous Turkish March, one of the most popular tunes that Beethoven ever wrote, but also a rather amazing and wild Chorus of Dervishes that's huge fun. Stick it on your sound system and challenge one of your theoretically knowledgeable friends to guess the composer. Beecham's version, although not complete, is pretty much unbeatable for the Dervishes alone.

These "chips off of the master's workbench" are perfect if you can find them as digital downloads. Otherwise, you might want to check out either Dausgaard's set of Beethoven's complete orchestral music, happily

Interlude 2 123

available in separate volumes, or acquire one of the several complete Beethoven editions being offered in connection with his 250th birthday celebrations. Some of these probably will be broken up and released as a series of individual boxes, including, hopefully, one devoted to the stage music. Because we already have discussed the overtures in some detail, the only remaining question is just how deeply you want to explore the inner recesses of Beethoven's output. I wouldn't consider this music an urgent acquisition. Call it a project for a rainy day.

Part 4

Symphonies

Discography (listed by orchestra/conductor)

Symphonies (complete cycles):
Cleveland Orchestra/George Szell
NDR Symphony Orchestra/Günter Wand
Royal Liverpool Philharmonic or Scottish Chamber
  Orchestra/Charles Mackerras
Staatskapelle Berlin/Daniel Barenboim
Leipzig Gewandhaus Orchestra/Herbert Blomstedt
Paris Conservatory Orchestra/Carl Schuricht

Symphony no. 1 in C Major, op. 21
Swedish Chamber Orchestra/Thomas Dausgaard
Deutsches Kammerphilharmonie Bremen/Paavo Järvi
Heidelberg Symphony/Thomas Fey
L'Orchestre de la Suisse Romande/Ernest Ansermet

Beethoven's Symphonies: Orchestration (in addition to strings and timpani)

Symphony Number	1	2	3	4	5	6	7	8	Wellington's Victory	9*
flutes	2	2	2	1	2	2	2	2	4	2
piccolo					1	1			2	1
oboes	2	2	2	2	2	2	2	2	4	2
clarinets	2	2	2	2	2	2	2	2	4	2
bassoons	2	2	2	2	2	2	2	2	4	2
contrabassoon					1					1
horns	2	2	3	2	2	2	2	2	8	4
trumpets	2	2	2	2	2	2	2	2	6	2
trombones					3	2			3	3
percussion									bass drum, cymbals, triangle, snare drums, ratchets, rifle and cannon shots	bass drum, cymbals, triangle

*plus solo vocal quartet and chorus

Symphony no. 2 in D Major, op. 36
Swedish Chamber Orchestra/Thomas Dausgaard
Deutsches Kammerphilharmonie Bremen/Paavo Järvi
Heidelberg Symphony/Thomas Fey
L'Orchestre de la Suisse Romande/Ernest Ansermet

Symphony no. 3 in E-flat Major (*Eroica*), op. 55
Philharmonia Orchestra/Otto Klemperer
NBC Symphony Orchestra/Arturo Toscanini (1953)
Concertgebouw Orchestra/Pierre Monteux
Deutsches Kammerphilharmonie Bremen/Paavo Järvi
Pittsburgh Symphony Orchestra/Manfred Honeck
Concertgebouw Orchestra/Erich Kleiber
NDR Symphony Orchestra/Klaus Tennstedt
London Symphony Orchestra/Leopold Stokowski

Symphony no. 4 in B-flat Major, op. 60
London Symphony Orchestra/Bernard Haitink
Vienna Philharmonic/Karl Bohm
Heidelberg Symphony/Thomas Fey
Philharmonia Orchestra/Otto Klemperer
Deutsches Kammerphilharmonie Bremen/Paavo Järvi
Berlin Philharmonic/Eugen Jochum

Symphony no. 5 in C Minor, op. 67
Berlin Philharmonic Orchestra/Lorin Maazel
Lamoureux Orchestra/Igor Markevitch
Pittsburgh Symphony/Manfred Honeck
Vienna Philharmonic/Carlos Kleiber
Concertgebouw Orchestra/Erich Kleiber (mono)
Vienna Philharmonic/George Szell (Orfeo, live)
Philharmonia Orchestra/Otto Klemperer

Symphony no. 6 in F Major (*Pastoral*), op. 68
Columbia Symphony Orchestra/Bruno Walter
Vienna Philharmonic/Karl Bohm
Philharmonia Orchestra/Otto Klemperer
Vienna Philharmonic/Pierre Monteux
Heidelberg Symphony/Thomas Fey
Orchestre de Paris/Rafael Kubelik

Symphony no. 7 in A Major, op. 92
Staatskapelle Dresden/Herbert Blomtstedt
Vienna Philharmonic/Leonard Bernstein
Royal Philharmonic Orchestra/Thomas Beecham
Pittsburgh Symphony/Manfred Honeck
New York Philharmonic/Arturo Toscanini (1936)
Berlin Philharmonic/Ferenc Fricsay
Marlborough Festival Orchestra/Pablo Casals
Chamber Orchestra of Europe/Nikolaus Harnoncourt

Symphony no. 8 in F Major, op. 93
London Symphony Orchestra/Bernard Haitink
Czech Philharmonic/Paul Kletzki
Swedish Chamber Orchestra/Thomas Dausgaard
Deutsches Kammerphilharmonie Bremen/Paavo Järvi
NBC Symphony Orchestra/Arturo Toscanini
Royal Philharmonic Orchestra/Hermann Scherchen
Marlborough Festival Orchestra/Pablo Casals

Wellington's Victory (*Battle Symphony*), op. 91
Minneapolis Symphony Orchestra/Antal Dorati
Cincinnati Symphony Orchestra/Erich Kunzel
Berlin Philharmonic/Herbert von Karajan (with *Egmont* incidental music)

Symphony no. 9 in D Minor (*Choral*), op. 125
Berlin Philharmonic/Ferenc Fricsay
Vienna Philharmonic/Hans Schmidt-Isserstedt
Philharmonia Orchestra/Wilhelm Furtwängler (Lucerne Festival, 1954)
Vienna Philharmonic/Karl Böhm (DG analogue)
Berlin Philharmonic/Herbert von Karajan
Berlin Philharmonic/Claudio Abbado (Sony Classical)
Boston Symphony Orchestra/Charles Munch
Deutsches Kammerphilharmonie Bremen/Paavo Järvi

Just a few brief remarks on the discography:

The first question that needs to be answered in purchasing recordings of the Beethoven symphonies is whether you should get a complete cycle, or individual discs. My suggestion, on the assumption that eventually you will want to acquire different performances of your special favorites, would be to start with one complete set (most of which are available at budget price) and then supplement as your time, finances, and enthusiasm permit.

I'd begin with either Szell or Wand, classics sets both, but you really can't go wrong with any of those listed. Charles Mackerras is a great choice if you prefer "historically informed" interpretations, albeit on much better-sounding, modern instruments. Daniel Barenboim offers performances in the romantic German tradition of his hero, Wilhelm Furtwängler, only unquestionably better played and recorded. I discussed the Schuricht performances in chapter 1—they are wonderful, but in mono—whereas Herbert Blomstedt's cycle with the Leipzig Gewandhaus Orchestra reflects a lifetime's consideration of this music by an underrated but truly masterful musician. Take your pick.

As to the recordings of individual works, the first two symphonies often come paired together, conveniently, and the selections reflect that. With one exception, all of them feature "historically informed" approaches to varying degrees, and the performances are quite simply as exciting as hell. Dausgaard's form part of a cycle of Beethoven's complete orchestral works for the Norwegian Simax label. The series is worth collecting but may be hard to source in its entirety. The exception to the "historically informed" paradigm is Ernest Ansermet, one of the podium giants of the first half of the twentieth century and yet another member of the French school who, in these works at least, proves that Beethoven never enjoyed a German monopoly.

In the later works, we find marvelous and distinctive interpretations covering a huge range of approaches. No Beethoven collection can be complete without some performances by Otto Klemperer, uniquely grand and granitic, and way too slow for some listeners (but not me). At the time of writing, some of the best recent Beethoven performances have been those by Paavo Järvi, in period style, and Manfred Honeck, a brilliant conductor working with the world-class Pittsburgh Symphony. All of his discs are worth hearing, whether of Beethoven or anyone else. Another essential release for collectors is the earliest recording included here: Toscanini's 1936 Seventh Symphony with the New York Philharmonic. You have to put up with limited sonics, but for the historically minded this was the recording that effectively defined modern standards of orchestral execution and interpretation. The performance itself has held up amazingly well—from a purely musical point of view, it is timeless.

The Ninth Symphony is a world unto itself, and for that reason it has been recorded successfully by many conductors, such as Karajan or Abbado, whose Beethoven otherwise leaves me feeling pretty cold. Each of them has left multiple versions of the piece, and I have tried to choose the ones that strike me as the best of the lot. For much of the middle decades of the twentieth century, the Ninth's principal avatar was Furtwängler, who left behind many live recordings, most of which suffer from lousy sound, slipshod ensemble, or both. His interpretation is extremely personal, even eccentric, but unquestionably enthralling when it works, as it finally does in his 1954 Lucerne Festival recording with the Philharmonia Orchestra.

Some of the best versions of the Ninth (as with all of the symphonies, to be frank) come from conductors you might not have heard of. For decades one of the very greatest recordings, by universal consent, has been Hans Schmidt-Isserstedt's with a sensational lineup of soloists and the Vienna Philharmonic, which never played the piece better for anyone.

Finally, a quick word on *Wellington's Victory*. This is a "battle symphony" that, to be honest, no one really listens to for the actual music. What you want is a sonic blockbuster recording with every cannon shot and rifle volley securely in place, ideally blasted out at deafening volume from opposite stereo speakers. The Dorati and Kunzel recordings deliver the goods, but Karajan is worth considering if only because you get the *Egmont* incidental music as a coupling—and despite his efforts to sound profound, Karajan really was a great conductor of "lighter" music. Other versions abound, of course, but if you don't own the Dorati, originally recorded with incomparable care and vividness for Mercury Living Presence, then you really don't know the work.

I will mention some additional recordings from the lists in discussing the symphonies individually. Although I have strong personal preferences as regards interpretation, it's not my opinion that matters—it's yours. More than enough versions are listed here to permit you to make up your own mind by sampling the broad spectrum of legitimate and worthwhile conceptions of these inexhaustible musical treasures.

Symphonies Nos. 1 and 2

Symphony No. 1

Taken together, Symphonies nos. 1 and 2 belong to Beethoven's early period, although the Second clearly is on the way to bigger things. In fact, when they were written, in some senses he already had moved on. Listeners to Beethoven more generally, as opposed to just his symphonic works, always are struck especially by the relative conservatism of the First Symphony. This doesn't diminish its quality one bit, but it does permit us to consider a couple of factors, one personal, the other historical, that really do help us get a handle on what Beethoven was doing in his first symphonic efforts, and why.

The personal factor we need to consider is a surprising one, not usually mentioned in discussions of Beethoven. Initially at least, he was a very cautious composer. By the time he composed the First Symphony, he was nearly thirty. Although famous as a keyboard virtuoso, and already acquiring a reputation for being obnoxious, paranoid, or otherwise difficult, he was very careful not to step on the toes of his illustrious predecessors—Mozart, who had died only recently, in 1791; and Haydn, who was very much alive and, moreover, became his teacher. The list of major early works completed roughly between 1794 and 1799, the year of the First Symphony, is instructive:

Three Piano Trios, op. 1
Piano Sonatas nos. 1–10 (including the *Pathétique*)
Two Cello Sonatas, op. 5
Three String Trios, op. 9

Three Violin Sonatas, op. 12
Piano Concertos nos. 1 and 2
Six String Quartets, op. 18

Most of these show Beethoven working in areas that Mozart and Haydn either ignored entirely, or on which they had not staked their reputations. The first two piano concertos are exceptions justified entirely by Beethoven's own virtuoso credentials, making comparisons with Mozart's works in the medium largely irrelevant. But 1799 was a breakthrough year, because in the op. 18 String Quartets and the First Symphony he threw down the gauntlet, to Haydn especially, but he did so very unequally. The string quartets, private works for sophisticated music lovers, are in every way more musically advanced than the avowedly public symphony. You can hear this immediately for yourself when listening. Or just spend twenty minutes with the *Pathétique* Piano Sonata of 1798, music of an intensity and expressive depth that Beethoven wouldn't attempt in orchestral music until the Third Piano Concerto several years later (incidentally in his same "personal" key of C minor).

The historical factor concerns the medium of the symphony itself. It was Haydn who made the symphony a major attraction, especially in his twelve works composed for London between 1791 and 1795. Even so, concerts featuring symphonies had to include other, often more audience-grabbing attractions: a major vocal or instrumental soloist, or an audience participation event. It was very common, for example, for a virtuoso to ask audience members to suggest tunes on which to improvise large fantasias on the spot. "Circus freaks" also were popular, in the form of child prodigies, or performers on strange instruments such as Marianne Kirchgessner, a blind glass-harmonica player celebrated in Vienna (Mozart wrote his Adagio and Rondo K. 617 for her).

In these surroundings, symphonies often went by their alternative designation, "overture," for that's what they were: curtain-raisers, interludes, and light diversions designed to fill the time between the main events. They could be played in sections, movements excerpted or substituted, and generally treated with less seriousness and integrity than they deserved. Their music, too, was expected to be light and mostly jolly. Mozart and Haydn began to take them into deeper expressive waters, but it was Beethoven who completed the process, not without controversy. The First Symphony certainly was not a major step in this direction, but it would be a mistake to call it shallow or immature for this reason. The fact that Beethoven didn't pull out all the stops, symphonically speaking, from day one doesn't lessen the music's polish, craftsmanship, or appeal one bit. The music is full of specifically Beethovenish elements, albeit introduced in genial, even comic contexts.

I already have mentioned the wonderfully sly introduction, with its harmonic tricks (it begins with an ending) and delicious orchestration for woodwinds and pizzicato strings. A lot of previous symphonies start with slow introductions, but none quite like this. The remainder of the first movement bounces along with energetic good humor, but one telling moment seems to foreshadow something of the expressive depth to come. At the end of the second subject, a perky tune for oboe, a sudden shadow hovers over the music as the melody passes to the lower strings, gliding along smoothly for a moment of reflection before rising quickly back to the sunny surface. Thus, we learn that the symphony's humorous demeanor is entirely purposeful and does not stem from Beethoven's inability to explore the expressive alternatives.

The slow movement features what I can only characterize as an almost insolent mastery of form and expression. It starts with a joke that sounds like it wants to be a fugue. The various string sections enter one after the other, but it turns out that they're only playing a game of catch-up, uniting for the main theme's latter half, which also doubles as its own "motion music." This allows the second subject to begin succinctly, as soon as the first has ended, with no need for additional transitional material. Written in textbook sonata form, each of the initial sections—first and second subjects with a full exposition repeat if taken—comes to a complete close, so Beethoven makes certain that you know exactly where you are.

Listen for the quiet rhythmic entry of trumpets and timpani at the exposition's very end. This rhythm carries over into the development, which otherwise consists almost entirely of increasingly pensive repetitions of the initial theme's first two or three notes. It seems as if it could go on forever—that is, until the omnipresent rhythm of the trumpets and drums makes a threatening gesture, and the orchestra, somewhat flustered at first, initiates the recapitulation.

Beethoven still calls the third movement a "Menuetto," but it's not. This is the world's first symphonic scherzo: faster, lighter, and rhythmically unpredictable. The central trio section gives the woodwind section a chance to shine with a "melody" consisting of little more than repeated chords. Beethoven's treatment of the winds generally in this symphony still is relatively restrained, solo oboe excepted. You'd hardly know that the work uses clarinets at all. This will change pretty quickly, but for now he's still scoring mostly for strings, with occasional washes of color from the other orchestral departments.

The finale begins with another joke, as the strings try to remember how the main tune is supposed to go. Their apparent amnesia becomes only more amusing when we realize that what they're forgetting is a simple rising scale. The music's high spirits only increase through the ensuing motion music on the lower strings and a second subject that's one of the breeziest tunes Beethoven ever wrote. The development section ends with a bounce, and we also get a very funny coda in which everyone lets us know that they now have no problem playing the opening theme's initial rising scale.

In sum, if this symphony isn't "deep" Beethoven and offers no special challenges or revolutionary innovations in terms of form or expression, third movement perhaps excepted, it is a perfect little gem by an already very experienced composer.

Symphony No. 2

Some readers may have had the good fortune of coming across Nicolas Slonimsky's *Lexicon of Musical Invective*, one of the most amusing and instructive books on music ever published. Among its delightful selection of reviews trashing famous works by master composers from Beethoven to Stravinsky, we find this contemporary notice about the Second Symphony:

> Beethoven's Second Symphony is a crass monster, a hideously writhing wounded dragon, that refuses to expire, and though bleeding in the Finale, furiously beats about with its tail erect.

This reaction might come as a surprise to modern listeners, especially those who consider Symphony no. 2 to be relatively immature, "light" Beethoven, but that contemporary critic recognized something important that we would do well to bear in mind: this newcomer offers music on another scale entirely from that of the First Symphony—bolder, grittier, and, above all, more subversive.

Indeed, the Second Symphony was the largest and grandest work of its kind yet written when it first appeared in 1802, a fact we are apt to forget in considering its monumental successor. It reveals at every point Beethoven's intention to expand the scope and seriousness of the medium, even though the music's overall demeanor remains generally happy and contented. As the review above shows, not everyone applauded this effort, which becomes obvious right from the start. Like the First Symphony, the Second begins with a slow introduction, but this one is huge—more than two and a half minutes, which is long enough to leave us questioning whether something different is still to come or we are listening to an independent movement.

As this slow first section proceeds, it gradually becomes evident that we are, in fact, listening to an introduction. See if you can put your finger on the moment when the music ceases to be self-contained or proclamatory and begins to arouse our expectations that something new is waiting down the road. It offers no direct anticipations of the Allegro that follows; Beethoven achieves his shift in emphasis entirely through the introduction's own melody, rhythm, texture, and harmony. Moreover, this big opening paragraph doesn't come to a firm close or end on the usual pregnant pause. Its accumulated momentum carries straight over into the main body of the movement, a steady increase of tension that characterizes Beethoven's strategy more generally.

For example, many symphonic expositions feature a bold, "masculine" theme for the first subject, then subside into a contrasting lyrical, softer, "feminine" second subject. This is what happens, more or less, in the First Symphony. Not here. The first subject is a quiet theme on lower strings with rapid violin figurations above, and the tension only increases with some highly agitated motion music that passes through a turbulent minor key. The second subject, when it finally arrives, is a march led by the clarinets (making their Beethoven symphonic debut in a leading role), punctuated by loud outbursts from the full orchestra. Again, the tension and energy keep rising, so it should come as no surprise that this second subject includes a bold "Beethoven bounce" among its concluding gestures.

Once you know this music really well, and by this I mean well enough to have both the first and second subjects so firmly in your memory that you can compare them mentally, you may notice a wonderful subtlety: the second subject is actually a variant of the first. Their relatedness, at first perhaps perceived only subconsciously, gives the entire movement a very satisfying, organic cohesion, which is important because at about eleven minutes in a typical performance it's unusually substantial for its period. Indeed, the entire symphony will last longer than half an hour, longer than the Fifth in most cases, and six or seven minutes longer than the First, which gives you some idea of its unprecedented scale. This is where that "dragon" moniker undoubtedly comes from.

Beethoven marks the second movement "Larghetto." The "etto" suffix in Italian is a diminutive, so it could mean a "small largo," which this most certainly is not. Often, it lasts even longer than the first movement. On the other hand, "etto" can also mean "a little bit," which has the effect of slowing down quick movements and speeding up slow ones. Hence, "allegretto" is "a little bit quick," or slower than plain "allegro," and "larghetto" would mean "a little bit slow," and so faster than mere "largo." Look for performances, then, where this Larghetto takes about the same time, give or take a minute or two, as the first movement. Although very lyrical in mood, and incredibly beautiful melodically, the music has plenty of variety and should never sound completely static.

Formally speaking, although the movement is in sonata form, it never makes a point of the fact, unlike the slow movement of the First Symphony with its first subject, second subject, and closing theme allocated to three distinct tunes. Here, in contrast, Beethoven liberally spreads a broad range of ideas—around half a dozen or so, depending on how you count them—over the entire exposition. Once again, the clarinet has an important solo part, this time in presenting the first subject. It has no exposition repeat, as a result of which the development section is very extensive. Because Beethoven presents such an abundance of material that you only get to hear once in the exposition, the best way to listen is just to relax and let the entire chain of tunes pass by in succession, taking on different expressive affects as the music proceeds and some of them are repeated or developed.

The third movement Scherzo finally is called that, and you never could mistake it for a minuet. Although strictly flowing in three beats to the bar, the way Beethoven breaks up the melody between orchestral sections, with both the colors and the volume changing almost with every measure, makes it sound curiously lopsided. No way are you going to dance to this music, vigorous and muscular though it is. The same observation holds true for the Trio section, which contains its own share of surprises. This isn't a long movement at all, maybe a bit more than four minutes on average, but the wide range of incident makes it sound bigger than it really is.

Beethoven's first big symphonic rondo follows his standard form: ABACABA, with the middle section (C) in a minor key and here doing double duty as a development section as well. The ritornello theme (A) is very eccentric, positively cartoonish in fact, and wonderfully contrasted with the suave motion music that immediately follows on the cellos, with the violas and second violins in dialogue. For a second subject (or episode B), Beethoven finds a simple melody in long, descending four-note phrases for the winds over a gently chugging string accompaniment. It has a tendency to move into minor keys, giving it a thoughtful, almost melancholy quality at times.

This is the entire substance of an often-hilarious movement, nowhere more so than when we happily encounter the very first of Beethoven's "codas that just won't quit" at the end. This must be the bit where the wounded dragon "refuses to expire, and though bleeding in the Finale, furiously beats about with its tail erect." You can't say that Beethoven's early critic failed to understand what the music was doing—he just objected to the entire concept as a matter of principle. Among the most entertaining of the rapid sequence of jokes in this endlessly "erect" coda is the fact that the development of the previous motion music happens along the way, the orchestra evidently having forgotten to do it earlier, where it more properly belonged.

Although only a couple of years separate Beethoven's first two symphonies, you can easily hear the major developments in style that occurred between them. Many Beethoven scholars place the major leap in his symphonic development between the Second and Third Symphonies, if only because the *Eroica* is so huge and so obviously striving to be taken much more seriously. Its differences are in plain sight, as it were. In my view, however, Beethoven crossed his first major bridge between Symphonies nos. 1 and 2, and the *Eroica* builds on what he already had achieved here in his wonderfully lucid, ebullient, and funny second effort in the medium.

Symphonies Nos. 3 (*Eroica*) and 4

Symphony No. 3 (*Eroica*)

Beethoven's *Eroica* Symphony is a magnificent, earth-shattering masterpiece, often hailed as the first great work of musical romanticism. It explores extremes of feeling—of heroism, strife, triumph, grief, and exaltation—on a volcanic scale unheard of in previous orchestral music. As I mentioned in the preface, despite the work's epochal significance, it's not one of my favorites, though I confess to enjoying it thoroughly in a great performance. Happily, quite a few of them have been recorded, George Szell's perhaps first among them, with Manfred Honeck's more recent version fabulous enough to restore one's faith in humanity.

Still, for me the work presents genuine challenges to both performers and listeners that I propose to describe, not to justify my own personal taste (or lack of it), or to plaster graffiti on a monument of Western musical culture but, rather, to lay out the issues plainly in such a way that you can use them as opportunities to engage positively and constructively with some of the specific questions that this very serious, provocative music raises. This angle strikes me as a useful way to consider a work so frequently mythologized and taken for granted that it's difficult to approach with the necessary clarity and objectivity.

I divide the following discussion about the symphony into two basic categories: questions about the music itself, including a movement-by-movement description, and sources of confusion arising from the way it often has been viewed and written about in the popular literature. This second category, which is where we will begin, is important to cover because you can't get away from it. Read any program note, or purchase any recording, and you'll likely have to contend with some aspects of the "*Eroica* myth," most of them highly misleading. It will help in describing the actual music, then, to clear the air and dispel some of the more usual claims about it that tend to do more harm than good when listening.

Category I: Problems with the *Eroica* Myth

1. The first subject of the symphony's opening movement is a primal motive based on the three notes of the fundamental chord of its home key, E-flat major. We do not hear the entire theme at once. Rather, it appears three times separated by increasing levels of agitation before, on its third attempt, it finally bursts out loudly in the full orchestra. These disruptive elements consist of, first, harmonies foreign to the home key; and, second, strongly syncopated rhythms that cut across the music's basic 3/4 time signature. As Leonard Bernstein pointed out in one of his typically astute talks, Beethoven is telling us right from the start that the music will be "about" the conflict between the pure harmony of the theme and the efforts to get away from or otherwise oppose it.

All of this is perfectly clear when listening. However, you're much more likely to read some remark such as Tovey's about the first foreign element that Beethoven interjects, the note C-sharp in the cellos and basses (followed by a series of syncopated Gs on the violins). Tovey calls this alien harmony a "cloud" and advises us in his discussion (published in *Essays in Musical Analysis*), "Whatever you may enjoy or miss in the Eroica Symphony, remember this cloud; it leads eventually to one of the most astonishing and subtle dramatic strokes in all music." This turns out to be the fact that later, in the recapitulation, the harmony briefly resolves in a different direction. Is this the big deal that Tovey insists it is? I strongly doubt it. Nonetheless, this claim has been witlessly parroted by generations of lazy music writers and commentators, sending listeners on a frustrating "wild cloud chase" across the length and breadth of the first movement in search of the promised astonishment. Really, life is too short.

2. The next issue concerns the arrival of the same movement's recapitulation, where the principal horn softly intones a bit of the main

theme while the violins are sustaining the "wrong" harmony; it is a dissonant clash so soft and gentle to modern ears as to be completely unnoticeable, but it excited the ire and shock of so many contemporary listeners that some conductors corrected the harmony to make things "right." Discussions of this passage strike me as the biggest waste of time in all of the reams of nonsense written about this symphony. We cannot listen with the ears of our ancestors. Telling us how some of them might have reacted, although interesting historically, does nothing to further our understanding or appreciation of Beethoven's expressive intentions. Either the passage sounds shocking to us or it does not; and if it does not, we must find our shocks elsewhere.

3. Then there is the "new tune in the development" business. This conundrum usually takes the form of a question: "Why did Beethoven take the radical step of introducing an entirely new melody into the second half of the first movement's development section?" Usually we get no answer. It's a mystery arising out of the depths of Beethoven's unfathomable genius. However, if you've been paying attention to what has been going on up to that point, it is no mystery at all. The first subject is a simple motive based on the notes of a major chord. The second subject is no less rudimentary, and just as tiny: an island of quiet, repeated notes in dialogue between woodwinds and strings. It's over before you know it. Neither constitutes what we normally would call a melody. Beethoven clearly needs one. The only question is where to put it.

To answer, we need to consider an even more basic issue. If both the first and second subjects are small and, for this and various other reasons, not especially useful for purposes of development, then of what does one of the largest and most complex structures in the entire symphonic literature consist? The answer is "motion music." Tons of it. In fact, this movement contains many quite arresting themes and ideas, but they mostly form part of its transitional material. That is what gives the music its unprecedented "revolutionary" energy—its restlessness and confrontational attitude.

For example, the development section begins with the motion music that occurs between the first and second subjects, combining it with the "heroic" opening tune and later still more of the exposition's transitional ideas. In the first half of the development, these themes plunge headlong into a crisis in the form of a huge, dissonant pileup—a musical train wreck if ever there was one. It's based mainly on the disruptive, syncopated rhythms that precede the initial loud outburst of the first subject. Beethoven's new tune, plaintive and lyrical, lovely and heartfelt, arrives immediately afterward as the perfect contrast and emotional reaction to this violent catastrophe. It is exactly the right thing in the right place, neither mysterious nor unfathomable—rather, inevitable, as I'm sure you'll agree.

4. Finally, the first movement has a controversial performance practice issue that I should mention. The climax of the coda consists of the main theme blasted out by the trumpets, except that the valveless, natural instruments of Beethoven's day lacked the notes for the tune's second phrase. Until recently, conductors corrected this automatically by having our modern trumpets play the complete tune. Leaving it out sounds just terrible—like an accompaniment missing its melody, which is exactly what it is. The poor woodwinds, suddenly left to themselves in this context, haven't a chance. However, the "historically informed" folks often insist on playing the passage just as Beethoven wrote it, a horrible and musically indefensible decision.

However, this question has become part of the "*Eroica* myth," with some performers claiming that the trumpets' sudden disappearance represents the "defeat of the hero." This, in turn, prepares us to mourn his death in the ensuing Funeral March. Never mind the fact that it isn't the tune that vanishes, merely its audibility, or that the remainder of the movement concludes with music of unalloyed triumph.

Category II: General Musical Issues and Movement Descriptions

1. The first problem on initial encounter with the Third Symphony, in my opinion, concerns the balance between its various movements. We already have seen how, in most classical works in large forms, the biggest, or most intellectually dense, movement comes first, with the rest revealing a progressive loosening of structure and relaxation of expressive intensity. Indeed, in Beethoven's concertos it's not unusual

for the opening movement to last longer than the remaining two combined. The *Eroica* follows this pattern, which works very well when the subject matter is primarily sunny, even comedic in character; but given both the extraordinary length and emotional intensity of the first two movements (lasting more than half an hour combined), you can be forgiven for feeling that the last two (less than twenty minutes) don't quite measure up.

This presents a legitimate conceptual issue. If the first movement presents the victory of the hero, or the triumph of heroism, and the victor dies in the second movement, then you may well ask what the Scherzo and Finale are for. What are they supposed to represent? After all, the man already is dead, and neither movement qualifies as a convincing picture of some projected metaphysical or transcendental afterlife.

We must allow that Beethoven was surely right, especially after the desperately tragic, sustained darkness of the Funeral March second movement, to give his listeners an emotional break. The question then becomes whether he offers a contrast of the most effective kind.

Despite their being relatively brief when heard in context, you can't argue that the symphony's last two movements are in any way undersized or insubstantial. Indeed, compared to the two previous symphonies, both are much larger. The Finale alone lasts about twelve minutes, longer than any other Beethoven finale before the Ninth.

However, the extremely large first two movements establish a certain expectation, if not of length, then of weight and expressive significance. Absolute timings are less an issue if the intensity is there, and joy can be just as powerful an expressive quality as misery. It could be that Beethoven had not yet learned to express happiness with the same depth and power that characterize his evocations of heroic striving, sorrow, and pathos. This isn't a crime. He would get there, and very soon, too, in his Fourth Symphony. Whether he manages it in the *Eroica* is a matter of opinion. The Finale, in particular, can come to sound effortful, as though emotional spontaneity has taken a backseat to the music's ostentatious cleverness.

2. The scoring of the *Eroica* also raises questions. I already mentioned the matter of the trumpets' inability to play the entire main theme in the

first movement coda, but this only points to a larger issue. The orchestra that Beethoven requires is essentially the same as in his previous symphonies, plus one extra French horn, making three in all. He uses this trio to excellent effect in the central Trio section (for once, appropriately named) in the Scherzo. Throughout the symphony, Beethoven treats the woodwinds with wonderful freedom and a truly poetic feeling for their individual tone colors—the oboe in the Funeral March, for example, or the flute to characterize one of the variations in the finale.

Elsewhere, however, especially in a less-than-stellar performance, the scoring can sound thin, as if the music is bigger than its instrumental setting permits. Several moments I could point to illustrate this contention: the big pileup in the first movement development section; the tremendous fugue in the Funeral March's second episode; and particularly the Finale's "coda that just won't quit," with its brass parts that come and go and those oddly scrawny closing chords. The use of "authentic instruments" usually only makes the music sound even scrappier.

In his later symphonies, Beethoven solved this problem either by increasing the size of the orchestra more substantially than he does here, as in the Fifth and Sixth Symphonies, or finding ways of spacing the musical lines so as to create a fuller and often more powerful sonority, even when he has fewer instruments on hand (the Fourth and Seventh). Late romantic conductors such as Gustav Mahler, who were notorious tinkerers when it came to orchestration, had no compunction about rescoring passages they regarded as insufficiently effective. We scoff at this practice now, but it's only fair to acknowledge that they were trying to solve what they saw as a real problem—a genuine disparity between what the music wanted to express and its medium for doing so. Interestingly, one of the most scandalously interventionist podium masters of all in this regard, Leopold Stokowski, played the symphony surprisingly straight, making it sound glorious in the process.

3. Now let's say a few words about the symphony's four movements individually.

The opening Allegro usually lasts about fifteen minutes. Here's how its interior timings typically break down—I've selected George Szell's iconic recording with the Cleveland Orchestra for this example:

First Movement Total Timing: 14'50"
Exposition: 3'14"
Development: 5'16"
Recapitulation: 3'18"
Coda: 3'02"

As you can see, the longest section by far is the development, a fact remarkable in itself. However, if the conductor observes the exposition repeat (the above performance does not), the proportions change pretty radically, and many feel that the music works best without it. How its inclusion affects perception of the entire movement will naturally differ from one listener to the next. What is beyond doubt, however, is that the exposition flows beautifully into the development, whereas the lead-back to the start is one of Beethoven's most perfunctory and least persuasive—just a couple of abrupt chords coming out of nowhere. Nonetheless, it has become very common today to observe the repeat, making the first movement several minutes longer still.

However unconvincing it might sound initially, you might argue that this practice has two advantages. First, it never hurts to have the chance to rehear the movement's main material before moving on to the development, especially one so lengthy. Second, the first movement will be followed by a massive, slow Funeral March. This can last anywhere from fifteen to about eighteen minutes, on average. Szell takes 15'38". And it's not just a matter of timing. Those fifteen minutes or so contain the most emotionally harrowing, some might say spiritually exhausting, orchestral music that Beethoven ever wrote. Spending more time with quicker and livelier music might counterbalance the Funeral March's epic sorrow more effectively. I can't say for sure whether it does. Again, it's a question of personal choice and one's perception of specific performances.

The Funeral March itself is so huge, so varied, and so focused on the expression of shattering grief that it represents a world unto itself. Any difficulties on an initial encounter have less to do with matters of form than with the sheer length of its diverse sections and their often emotionally harrowing content. The good news is that the better you get to know it, the shorter it sounds. The music follows a very simple rondo design:

A: The main march theme, shuffling along in heavy, broken rhythms, with the lower strings imitating riffs on the parade drums
B: A lyrical, contrasting major-key episode culminating in a "bounce-like" fanfare
A: March reprise
C: Fugue, one of the grimmest, most rugged, and most powerful in the repertoire
A: March, but just a tiny fragment
D: Sudden interruption of alarming trumpet fanfares over striding strings
A: Final return of the full march above a fluttering accompaniment in the flutes and violins, broadening out into a very large "coda that just won't quit," at last subsiding into darkness

The way this march is played can make or break a performance. Too slow and too heavy, and it not only risks becoming merely boring, but it makes the next two movements sound even more irrelevant than they otherwise would. It has to move at a real march tempo, rhythmic and purposeful, however broken backed the music sounds. Done properly, it will have the desired devastating emotional impact, while permitting the Scherzo and Finale their welcome and refreshing contrast (Arturo Toscanini, George Szell, Pierre Monteux, Otto Klemperer, Manfred Honeck, and Erich Kleiber strike me as especially impressive in this regard).

Moving on to the Scherzo, you'd never mistake its swift accompaniment patterns as in any way deriving from the traditional minuet. Its principal theme hovers above in the woodwinds like a dancing ray of sunshine, only to burst out with muscular vigor in the full orchestra. The central Trio section is a hunting scene for the three horns, looking forward to the similar music in the Scherzo of the *Pastoral* Symphony. When the opening music returns, Beethoven plays with our expectations by alternating between triple and duple rhythms and concludes by adding a substantial coda led off by solo timpani. The entire piece offers a remarkable display of orchestral virtuosity. Emotionally speaking, it seems to walk a fine line between high spirits and something else entirely—a breathless energy bordering on the dangerous.

Symphonies Nos. 3 (Eroica) and 4

Taken on its own, the Finale undeniably represents an impressive achievement. Its shape basically is a theme with variations, including two intricate fugal episodes, but the form is not at all strict. The movement can be broken down into four main sections:

1. After the orchestra opens with a brief whirlwind of sound, we hear—not the theme—but rather its bass line in pizzicato strings. We don't know yet that this isn't the real theme; but with its bare scoring and odd pauses, it definitely sounds strange, even a touch grotesque, so it qualifies as a sort of "variation before the fact." Like the theme, its bass line has two halves, both repeated, although Beethoven writes out the first half repeat to bring in the woodwinds, making a very comical impression. Two further simple variations follow—in other words, they keep the shape of the bass line, with repeats intact, adding only some contrapuntal decorations around it.

Finally, the real theme sails in on the woodwinds—the famous tune that Beethoven couldn't get out of his head from the Twelve Contradances previously mentioned in our discussion of his ballroom music. The full orchestra celebrates this new discovery, and a tiny codetta brings these first three variations plus the theme to an open-ended conclusion. Beethoven's ingenious idea of only introducing the true theme after a few preludial variations had an interesting later influence on Rachmaninov's popular *Rhapsody on a Theme of Paganini*, which similarly begins with a skeletal preliminary variation before we hear the famous tune on which it's based.

2. From this point on, the course of the variations is very free and endlessly inventive. First, the bass line becomes the subject of a fugue, discussed for some time before the dance tune tries to return in its original form. This attempt quickly evaporates, leaving the solo flute to finish the variation. Next, a short orchestral interlude introduces a boldly striding, minor-key variant of the tune in the form of a march, leading to an emphatic closing gesture. But, no—once again the melody reappears, and once again the texture swiftly thins out, leading to a new fugue on the subject of the original bass line, only now in a version turned upside down ("inverted"). This builds gradually to a big climax that brings us back, seemingly, to where we started as the orchestra comes to rest on an expectant pause.

3. The dance melody does indeed return, only this time as a touchingly nostalgic and sentimental oboe solo in a slower tempo (Poco Andante, which is somewhere between andante and adagio). This version of the theme wins the rest of the orchestra's approval, evidently, because it gets played in a last, grand statement, now very majestic and richly accompanied. It's a wonderful transformation. Our theme, it seems, has grown up and finally reveals its full potential. Maybe what Beethoven is saying in the *Eroica*'s Finale is this: "There's a little bit of the hero in all of us, no matter how simple or unassuming first appearances might suggest." If so, it's a noble message, one wholly in keeping with his egalitarian sentiments.

4. The remainder of the movement is all coda. It begins sweetly until the shadow of the Funeral March seems to infect the music with darker feelings, and anxiety intervenes. Palpitating woodwinds seem at a loss to know how to continue, when suddenly the movement's opening whirlwind interrupts with a shout, and the music races on to its jubilant close. Notice that what sounds like a new theme in the horns is nothing more than the first four notes of the principal dance tune.

If I feel conflicted about the fitness of the Finale as the conclusion of the entire symphony's emotional journey, this and all of the issues just discussed depend for their successful resolution on the conductor's interpretation. A great performance banishes all doubt. Szell's account of the Finale, for example, is thrilling, and his coda never has been equaled in its energy, precision, and satisfying sense of completion. He focuses your attention wholly on what Beethoven wants to express.

Nevertheless, for the very real problems that the music presents to both players and audiences, the *Eroica* strikes me as the most difficult of all of the Beethoven symphonies to perform successfully and, conversely, the one most likely to fail—especially when it is taken for granted because it's no longer particularly difficult technically for today's players. This is perhaps the biggest crime of all. If the symphony is "about" anything, it's about *struggle*, a quality that you hear and experience at many levels simultaneously: in the music's emotional expression, naturally, but also in its execution and interpretive challenges. It should never sound merely easy.

The shadow that passes over the music in the coda of the Finale, just when you think that all has been said and done to our complete satisfaction, conveys an especially striking message in this respect. It tells us that victory is not a given but must be won through vigorous and continued effort. Although performances of the *Eroica* in concert are frequent, ones that imaginatively grapple with the formal and expressive issues that the symphony raises are very rare. For that reason, I almost always enjoy hearing it more on recordings, where I can pick and choose among the versions that affect me most powerfully and listen without distraction.

Symphony No. 4

The Fourth Symphony hasn't been eulogized in the same way as has the *Eroica*, but it was the subject of at least one silly statement, by Robert Schumann as it turns out, who called it "a slender Greek maiden between two Norse giants." Of course, had he replaced the term "two Norse giants" with "two hefty German Hausfraus," our view of the work would be considerably different. A more accurate description might be "an Olympic sprinter between two sumo wrestlers," because this more aptly describes Beethoven's fit, trim, fleet, and muscular Fourth Symphony as it relates to its bulker companions; but even this wouldn't quite be correct for, in fact, it usually lasts longer than the Fifth Symphony, believe it or not.

However we choose to describe it, the Fourth represents a considerable advance over the Third, both musically—and, I would argue—even expressively. This is the work in which Beethoven discovered how to treat joyous feelings with the same depth and subtlety that characterized his prior evocation of sadness in places such as the *Eroica*'s Funeral March. The fact that the symphony lasts only about thirty-three to thirty-five minutes, and is considerably more compact in other respects, too, changes nothing. This will become very evident if we consider the work in light of some of the same points that we raised in discussing its more illustrious predecessor, as well as explore some of its unique features.

Balance of Movements

None of the Fourth Symphony's individual movements is unusually lengthy, but the question of balance between them, as previously mentioned, has as much to do with intensity of expression as it does raw playing time. In this respect the Fourth definitely breaks new ground. Although it has no movements in a minor key, the range of emotion within them and the level of moment-to-moment contrast have increased noticeably, a fact highlighted by the work's comparative brevity.

The Scherzo even represents an instance of formal expansion. Instead of the standard ABA, Beethoven now makes the scherzo and trio come around twice: ABABA. This not only brings the length of the movement more into line with its surroundings, but it "sonatafies" the music by playing with the listener's sense of time. We don't know how often the music will return, and to keep from feeling that we're stuck in a sort of endless loop, Beethoven needs to arrange a dramatic, last-minute exit. The result intensifies the music's humor and forces the composer to increase its interest more generally, so the repetitions don't become tiresome.

It also reveals Beethoven's desire to achieve a better balance between the work's individual parts. Compare this to the *Eroica*, where the Scherzo, although bigger than this example, lasts only about a third as long as either of the first two movements and half the length of the finale. Here, on the other hand, the Scherzo is more than 50 percent the size of the main Allegro or the Adagio, and nearly equal to the finale's timing. Beethoven will play with this new strategy very happily in the Sixth, Seventh, and Ninth Symphonies as well.

Here, for purposes of comparison, is an outline of the symphony's movements in terms of their timings. The performance selected is Bernard Haitink's with the London Symphony Orchestra:

First Movement: 11'13", of which,
Introduction (Adagio): 2'25"
Allegro vivace: 8'48"
Second Movement (Adagio): 9'05"
Third Movement (Allegro vivace): 5'37"
Fourth Movement (Allegro ma non troppo): 6'47"

Scoring

The Fourth uses the smallest orchestra of any Beethoven symphony, requiring only a single flute, in addition to the usual pairs of woodwinds, horns, trumpets, and timpani with strings. Here's an interesting bit of history: many works written during the classical period, including symphonies by Haydn, Mozart, and some of Beethoven's piano concertos, ask for just one flute. Mozart reportedly hated the instrument. You would think that the poor creature, sitting all alone in the orchestra, would be completely overwhelmed by its colleagues, and, of course, in tutti passages this is true; but this tactic had a good reason.

Until a few decades into the nineteenth century, flute construction was completely unstandardized, even as regards instruments produced by the same manufacturer. With no set rule governing where the finger holes went, no two flutes played in tune with each other. The sound that they made together must have been excruciating. Therefore, it was safer and smarter to limit the scoring to just one flute if you could get away with it. Beethoven makes a virtue of the practice here, for every time the flute plays in lightly scored passages it effectively has a solo, and you can hear more of it in this symphony than in many others that require a larger complement.

Beethoven's scoring for woodwinds in this symphony generally has become completely free. Players have many famous passages they look forward to with great relish: the clarinet solo in the Adagio, the quizzical interjections for clarinet and bassoon in the Scherzo, or the virtuoso bassoon lead-back to the main theme in the Finale. The constantly changing colors give the music a characteristic shimmer that's very beautiful, and unique to this particular work. Beethoven is learning how to individualize his symphonies using instrumental timbre, not just for decorative effect but as a means of articulating his symphonic structures and jogging the listener's memory through sound alone.

For example, returning to the flute for a moment, you will notice that it has solos in the second subjects of both the first movement and finale. These may sound vaguely similar, melodically, linking the two movements together, but a big part of the reason we make the connection stems from the fact that the flute plays both passages. In fact, this symphony has many such links between the outer movements; the more you get to know the music, the more clearly you will notice them and the more cogent it will start to sound taken as a whole. No movement, in fact, could plausibly belong to another work, even if you can't put your finger on the exact reason why this is so. Instrumental timbre, in softer passages especially, plays a large part in creating this impression.

At high volume, Beethoven also has new things to say. Gone is the thinness that sometimes afflicted his writing in the *Eroica*. Part of the secret stems from his more imaginative use of the trumpets and timpani as regular participants in sustaining long chords and reinforcing inner parts. The result has a fullness of tone missing when these instruments are restricted to simple rhythms and military-type fanfares. Listen to the sledgehammer power with which Beethoven launches the first movement's main Allegro. This is loudness with meat on its bones, used to propel the music forward swiftly, athletically, with an almost effortless impulse.

Beethoven's New Gestural Vocabulary

A musical gesture is just what the word suggests: a signpost, an object. It could be based on a rhythm, a texture, a harmony, or some combination of these, but it's not a tune. A motive is a special kind of gesture, one usually incorporated into larger themes or melodies, but gestures often exist independently in addition to whatever motivic role they may play. The great master of the musical gesture in a symphonic context was Mahler; but the idea originated with Beethoven, and the Fourth Symphony is the work in which, more than any other, he discovered the power and flexibility of the gesture. It was something completely new in the vocabulary of music and, the *Eroica* notwithstanding, truly revolutionary.

Each movement of the Fourth employs a musical gesture (or two) in some way, and once you know what they are, you can follow them throughout the symphony easily and with great pleasure. For example, the principal gesture in the first movement is the short, sharp, repeated chord arising out of the big orchestral "shout" that leads off the Allegro (and concludes it as well). This primal idea launches the first subject like a rocket, dominates the development, and appears mysteriously at the start of the recapitulation separated by soft solo timpani rolls. It summarizes and projects the muscular energy and forward drive that characterize so much of this music, and you can't miss it. Think about it, though. It isn't a tune, or a recurring harmony, or texture. It's a jolt, a shake of the fist, an object with a definite shape—in short, a gesture.

The "Beethoven bounce" described in chapter 1 is a gesture, and the Adagio contains two of them. The first is the simple "dadum" rhythm that opens the movement and recurs throughout, sometimes as accompaniment and sometimes rising to the surface to take command of the proceedings. It can be either soft or loud, and appear at any time and in any instruments, including solo timpani at the very end. Used in this way, it provides the glue that binds together the movement's various episodes (it happens to be a very remarkable, slow rondo in full ABA-CABA form). The second bounce occurs at the end of the A section, or ritornello, and consists of a rolling, rising, and falling gesture for the full orchestra, like waves crashing regularly against the seashore.

This second bounce turns out to be capable of development, not within the movement but in the ones that follow. Each has its own equivalent. You can hear it at the end of the Scherzo's A section, with the rolling gesture swapped between the high and low instruments. In the finale, it occurs at the end of the exposition (and elsewhere), with a kind of chugging rhythm powered by dense chords and whirling strings. In all of these cases, the gesture usually involves the whole orchestra, at least when it appears at full volume. The version in the scherzo can be difficult to hear clearly unless the conductor takes special pains to bring out the figurations in the cellos and basses when they have them (Otto Klemperer is unmatched here). Beethoven's use of gestures thus turns out also to be a method for creating cyclical unity throughout the symphony without having to quote actual themes from one movement to the next. This turned out to be a very big deal in the Fifth Symphony, as you saw in our discussion of that work in chapter 2.

Richer Shades of Expression

The Fourth Symphony contains no movements in minor keys, and so its mood is primarily one of happiness and contentment, disturbed by only a passing shadow or two; and yet this simplistic description can't possibly capture the multiple shades of expression with which Beethoven invests the music.

Three examples provide evidence of the symphony's extraordinary (and new) range of feeling. The first must be the first movement's introduction—a passage that truly goes where no one has gone before. It is "space music" consisting of three elements: a sustained chord in the winds, an ominous string figure in long notes, and a sequence of clipped, detached (staccato) wind and string chords with brief pauses between them. From these building blocks, consisting almost entirely of texture without melody, Beethoven creates two and a half minutes of expectation. Nothing would be quite like it in music until the similar introduction at the start of Mahler's First Symphony.

The second example consists of the B section in the second-movement Adagio. This is a serene clarinet solo over isolated pizzicato strings, remarkable both for its lyrical beauty and its exceptional feeling of rapt stillness.

Finally, jump to the finale, with its perpetual motion figuration running through the strings almost throughout. We find something very similar in the *Prometheus* Overture, right down to the underlying rhythms, only here the basic idea travels through an entire landscape of shifting moods created by the constantly varied harmonies, textures, dynamics, and even speeds. I strongly urge you to make a real-time comparison of the two works—it's the difference between an innocent child and a worldly, experienced adult. It would only take you about twelve minutes, and you'd get the point immediately.

Finally, cyclical unity occurs among the symphony's principal themes, many of which can be shown to have originated in the music of the introduction. This is a complex and fascinating topic, about which a lot could be written. For our purposes, and to give you a head start, just remember the introduction's detached string and woodwind chords, speed them up in your head, and compare to the Allegro's first subject and the finale's transitional motion music (and second subject, which uses some of the same melodic shapes). What all of these ideas have in common is the same kind of even rhythm and staccato articulation, indicating that they belong to a single family, even if the actual melodies are different.

This, in turn, heightens the expressive character of the various themes by jogging our memory, allowing us to hear their transformations in different dramatic contexts, and encouraging us to make connections.

We have no need to explore this subject further. The better you know the music, the clearer details such as this come into focus. The point I want to stress is that the music hugely repays repeated listening. You will hear something new whenever you come back to it. Possibly because the Third and Fifth Symphonies are so obviously grander and perhaps emotionally more direct, the Fourth probably is the least popular—and certainly the least well understood of all of the Beethoven symphonies. However, the fact that its depths might be hidden to some extent doesn't mean that it doesn't have any; and it has much more in common with his later music than you first might assume.

Symphonies Nos. 5 and 6 (Pastoral)

Symphony No. 5

The Fifth Symphony already has been discussed extensively in chapter 2, so no need to do so again here. That said, I do want to mention two issues that are fun to think about when listening. Not only are they worth getting to know, but they might enrich your encounter with the music by giving you insider information about what happens in preparing the work for performance.

The Opening Bars

What could be simpler than Beethoven's iconic, twice-repeated, four-note opening motto: *short-short-short-long*? Believe it or not, this is one of the trickiest beginnings in the entire orchestral literature and one of the most difficult to conduct. Start with the long notes. These are sustained by what's known in the music business as a *fermata*, or "hold" sign. It looks like an upside down smiley with a dot in the middle, and it's usually placed above the note being held. Go ahead: look it up. Each of the long notes has one, except that the second has a fermata plus an extra half note tied to it. No one has any idea exactly what Beethoven meant by this, aside from the fact that the second long note should be held for more time than the first. But just how long is that?

The problem, you see, is that a fermata is an *unmeasured* pause. No rule dictates how long it should last. You could count it out for a definite number of beats, but that sort of defeats Beethoven's intention of giving the impression that time has, for a moment, stopped dead. Getting everyone to let go of the fermatas at the same time, as well as keeping the ensemble together when they move on, requires accomplished stick technique from the person on the podium. Performances in the first half of the twentieth century or those in the romantic tradition tend to hang on to the fermatas for a good while. More classically oriented or "historically informed" interpretations often prefer to keep the music moving with a minimum of disruption. One way sounds more portentous, the other more physically exciting right out of the gate.

This fermata stuff, however, doesn't hold a candle to the problems concerning the very first notes that you hear—the three quick ones leading to the one with the hold. You see, the symphony does not begin on the first beat. The time signature is 2/4, meaning two quarter-note beats to each measure. Those first three notes, however, aren't quarters, but eighths, and the first of them doesn't start on the very first beat, but half a beat later. In other words, the first "sound" of the symphony is an eighth rest's worth of silence. In a performance, you count eighth notes in 2/4 time measure by measure like this: *1-and-2-and*, *1-and-2-and*, and so forth. So, the first note you hear is the offbeat "and" after the 1.

Because the tempo is too quick for the conductor to beat the correct time in eighth notes, and most don't like to cheat by giving the orchestra a full empty bar ahead of the start to fix the desired tempo, it's an open question whether the strings and clarinets—which play these initial bars together—all will come in at the same time. Quite often, they don't. Again, it's a matter of podium technique (and preparation in rehearsal). This isn't usually an issue on studio recordings, which can take the time and trouble to get it right, but in concert or on recordings captured live, things can get interesting.

Some very major conductors, Wilhelm Furtwängler first among them, almost never got it right, and his performances of the Fifth often begin with the motto's three quick notes consisting of anywhere from four to six, depending on the circumstances. Furtwängler claimed not to care about precision of ensemble, at least in preference to weight of sonority and concern for the music's "spiritual" values; but I have to confess that I don't hear anything especially spiritual in a sloppy attack on the opening notes of Beethoven's Fifth. Others disagree. Furtwängler enjoys a cult following and has excited the admiration of many very important musicians, not least for his interpretations of this symphony.

Repeats in the Scherzo and Finale

As noted in the Fourth Symphony, Beethoven enlarged the Scherzo from the usual ABA to ABABA, a practice he also followed in the Sixth and Seventh Symphonies (and continued with a very cool fake-out maneuver in the Ninth). The Scherzo of the Fifth originally followed the same format, but Beethoven ultimately decided to eliminate the repeat. Some conductors, and at least one recent "critical edition," have restored it, although the vast majority respect what appear to be Beethoven's final thoughts and leave it out. The question I pose to you is this: Why did Beethoven cut the repeat?

Arguments for its inclusion include the fact that the Scherzo's A section is very short and has no internal repeats, so hearing it one more time can't hurt. Letting the Scherzo and Trio come around twice gives Beethoven's highly imaginative, spooky recasting of the A section on its third and final appearance greater impact because it's even more unexpected. On the other hand, you could argue that the Scherzo (but not the Trio) is, in fact, repeated—in the middle of the Finale. It may be that Beethoven felt that playing the same music multiple times beforehand reduced the impact of a moment that everyone agrees represents one of the great masterstrokes of surprise in all of music. Keeping the repeat also gives the Scherzo more independence as a separate movement simply by making it larger, whereas Beethoven's clear intention is that it should be joined to the Finale with both movements perceived as a single unit.

Perhaps even more than first movement expositions, which usually benefit from being heard twice, scherzo repeats are tricky things. The main sections of a scherzo usually consist of two halves, both repeated, so although the basic from is ABA, what you usually hear if all of the repeats are observed is AABBCCDDAABB, with C and D being the two halves of the Trio section, also with repeats. This very quickly can start to sound excessively long, and until the recent arrival of the "historically informed" folks, repeats in the reprise of the A section after the Trio would be omitted as a matter of course. Thanks to modern scholarship letting us hear the difference, we now know for sure that in most cases they still should be.

Finally, another repeat issue in the Fifth is worth mentioning—that of the Finale's exposition. The reason for controversy here is that the first movement already is quite short; and as we described previously, Beethoven has weighted the work toward the Finale anyway. Under these circumstances, observing the repeat can seem a bit like overkill, especially if the performance of the last movement is unusually noisy and manic. Determining your own preference requires that you hear the entire symphony straight through, because it's a matter of overall balance as well as a function of the evolving pattern of tension and relaxation in a specific interpretation. Try listening to the Finale in isolation, then in its proper context. You'll be amazed at how differently the music strikes you.

Symphony No. 6 (*Pastoral*)

The *Pastoral* Symphony remains a personal favorite for a very simple reason: it's the piece that turned me on to classical music. I was about six and just learning to read, so I was looking at labels and such around the house and trying to sound out the words that I saw. One object that caught my eye was my mother's recording of Beethoven's Sixth, with William Steinberg and the Pittsburgh Symphony on the long-defunct Command Classics label. The album cover reproduced a very famous painting, Pieter Breughel the Elder's *The Harvesters* (1565). I asked Mom what the word "pastoral" meant. She said, "Look at the cover." So I put the music on my toy record player, looked at the painting, and was blown away. I was hearing what I saw—the image and the music fit together perfectly. I had no idea why.

This was the moment I realized that music—just plain music, without words—could communicate specific feelings and evoke mental images directly, all by itself. The fact that it was "classical" was irrelevant, and in any case beyond my six-year-old understanding. All I knew was that the stuff *worked*. It spoke to me. It was like reading a book, watching a movie, or listening to a story, but somehow much more direct and personal because the musical message consisted of sound filtered through my own imagination—it was as if the work had been composed just for me. I have never tired of exploring the universe revealed to me on that day. This book contains some of what I have discovered.

I now know that I am not the only person to have had this experience, because something similar happens whenever you "get" a piece of music. It becomes a part of you in a way that no other kind of art or entertainment approaches. Music has no independent existence. It needs you, the listener, because its message does not lie merely in the abstract patterns of sounds generated by the performers but, rather, in the way you hear them and give them meaning. It could be that sentimental affection for a childhood memory leads me to say this, but I still feel that the *Pastoral* Symphony is special in the ease with which it allows listeners to enter and respond to its expressive world. I can think of no better introduction to symphonic music.

The fact that the music is programmatic—in other words, it's "about" some external subject that we know in advance—has nothing to do with its value in this regard. Richard Strauss's *Sinfonia Domestica* is as "about" as it gets. It describes a day in the life of his family, including giving the baby a bath, going to work, having sex with his wife, sleeping and dreaming, and ending with a rambunctious domestic dispute. We know all of this in advance, hear it moment by graphic moment, but (I suspect) we feel none of the immediate identification between sound and substance that happens when listening to the *Pastoral* Symphony. We even have some intriguing anecdotal evidence for the validity of this theory that I can share with you.

Giovanni Simone Mayr (aka Johann Simon, 1763–1845) was a German-born, naturalized Italian composer principally active in the town of Bergamo in Lombardy, where he established and ran a famous music conservatory. Although a major figure in his day, he has gone down in history principally as the teacher of the famous opera composer Gaetano Donizetti. Being German in orientation, he also was a huge admirer of Beethoven. Indeed, Mayr liberally helped himself to several of Beethoven's choicer ideas in his own orchestral works, including the opening of the Third Piano Concerto for the overture to the opera *The Americans* (*Gli americani*) and the second subject of the Second Symphony's opening movement in his Concerto Bergamasco for solo woodwinds and orchestra. All of these have been recorded (by Naxos) if you're curious.

When Beethoven died in 1827, Mayr immediately composed a memorial cantata that incorporated bits of the Beethoven works with orchestra that would have been most popular or familiar to contemporary audiences, or at least those in Bergamo. These references included three choices that practically no one especially enjoys or cares about today: the oratorio *Christ on the Mount of Olives*, the early Mass in C major, and the potboiler *Wellington's Victory*. The only music from any other piece by Beethoven consisted of extracts from the first and third movements of the *Pastoral* Symphony—not the *Eroica*, nor the Fifth, nor even the Ninth, whose vocal finale could have been counted on to appeal to the opera-loving Italians. No, it was the Sixth that Mayr chose to represent the outstanding example of Beethoven's symphonic legacy. It seems that something was special about it to listeners even then—qualities that we will consider now in greater detail.

The first point that needs to be made absolutely clear in connection with the *Pastoral* Symphony concerns what the music does and does not do. Beethoven said that the piece represents "more the expression of feeling than painting" (in tones). From this innocuous statement, legions of commentators have insisted that he preferred abstract over descriptive music, and consequently any such tone-painting, or programmatic content more generally, inherently was inferior. This imagined disparity became an amazingly vicious, all-out aesthetic war in the latter half of the nineteenth century, pitting partisans of program music, who idolized Wagner, against the defenders of pure, abstract music, epitomized by the works of Brahms. Both sides claimed historical justification for their position in the music of Beethoven.

However, let us take a moment to consider carefully Beethoven's own words. He did *not* say that the work contains no descriptive passages; only that, on balance, the expression of feeling took precedence over efforts at literal illustration in sound.

Now turn to the titles he gave the individual movements:

1. Awakening of happy feelings on arrival in the country
2. Scene by the brook

3. Merry gathering of country folk
4. Thunderstorm
5. Shepherd's song. Joyful and thankful feelings after the storm

Well, what do you know? Beethoven literally was right!

Two movement headings contain the word "feelings"; one, the "Merry gathering of country folk," characterizes the third movement in emotional terms as well. After all, music without words can't unambiguously portray "gathering country folk," but "merry" sentiments it can manage perfectly. Movements two and four, on the other hand, offer straightforward examples of painting in tones. They represent "things"—a pastoral scene by a brook, and a storm. So, yes, on balance, the symphony contains "more the expression of feelings than painting," arranged in a beautifully balanced, five-movement "arch" form, but it contains plenty of painting, too, and it's no less important or masterful than the rest.

Beethoven, in any event, makes no formal or technical distinction in his compositional approach between the two types of music. Both of his tone paintings employ sonata form, freely adapted to the music's poetic content in precisely the same manner as we find in his nondescriptive pieces. The symphony's outer movements include a sonata-form opener and a sonata-rondo finale. The central "merry gathering of country folk" is a scherzo and trio. As in the Fifth Symphony, Beethoven joins the latter movements together—three in this case, rather than two—creating a big block of continuous music that shifts the weight of the symphonic argument away from the opening movement, Beethoven's lightest in any event, and toward the finale.

As previously, the instrumentation supports the structure. Trumpets first appear in the Scherzo. Beethoven adds timpani, piccolo, and two trombones in the storm and retains the extra brass in the finale. The first movement's scoring for high horns and woodwinds, flutes especially, gives the piece an "open air," outdoors quality that reeks of the countryside. It's very similar to what Aaron Copland would do nearly a century and a half later to create the iconic sound of rural America and the Western prairie in his famous trio of ballets, *Billy the Kid*, *Rodeo*, and *Appalachian Spring*.

Clearly, for Beethoven the word "pastoral" meant something very specific in terms of the music's expressive content, and thanks to the movement titles we know exactly what this was. It's no mistake that the three parts concerned with the depiction of feelings include the adjectives "happy," "merry," and "joyful" in their headings. Beethoven's response to being in the countryside contains no misery. The two tone-paintings, however, capture nature's opposing forces of tranquility and violence in specifically musical terms: both the babbling brook and the thunderstorm make sounds in real life.

This is a very significant point. Sunsets, for example, are beautiful and often have been the subject of musical interpretation, but if the composer doesn't tell us "this is a sunset," then we have no way of matching the sounds to the image that inspired them. On the other hand, Beethoven's brook with its accompanying birdsong at the end, and later his thunderstorm, are self-explanatory. They are inherently musical, and so his stylized representation of them is every bit as "natural," and perhaps even more appropriate to the pastoral theme, than his theoretically purer, "abstract" portrayals of three degrees of happiness elsewhere.

One of the most outstanding characteristics of the *Pastoral* Symphony is the exceptional feeling of unity among the various movements. The entire work (one of Beethoven's longest) has a fulfilling sense of wholeness that has nothing to do with the mere technical fact of his linking together the last three sections. Once again, the movement titles provide a source of useful information. Specifically, the action of the symphony, all of it, takes place on "arrival in the countryside." Beethoven places all five movements in this singular location. How does he do it musically, especially given the remarkable fact that the movements share neither themes nor motives?

The most obvious tactic lies in evoking iconic sounds—not just the brook, literal birdsong, or the storm, but also the warbling flute in the first movement (stylized birdsong), the hunting horns in the Scherzo, and the shepherd's pipes at the start of the finale. All of these musical images tell us where we are; but Beethoven's technique is much more sophisticated than that. The Sixth Symphony makes very telling use of musical gestures, similar to those we discussed in considering the Fourth Symphony, but of a kind unique to this work. They consist, for the most part, of tiny groups of notes repeated continuously. For example, take the melody with which the symphony opens, drop the first three notes and isolate the next five (having the rhythm dum dadadum dum). Next, repeat this gesture endlessly but always inventively, using it to build up larger sections, accompany simple, folklike melodies, or create a dialogue between the various instruments.

Similarly, in the second movement, aside from the rippling brook portrayed by the strings (with two solo cellos), we hear a ubiquitous melodic fragment—a six-note "turn," tossed between the violins and solo woodwinds. Later, the Scherzo's hunting horn rhythm of vigorous, three-note figures becomes the accompaniment to the ensuing episode featuring a perky oboe melody (with a humorous bassoon commentary). In the finale, the motive of the shepherd's pipes returns like a refrain above and beyond the basic rondo structure of ABACABA, eventually concluding the whole symphony as a solo for muted horn. The use of simple gestures reinforced by repetition, combined with pure harmonies and primal, folklike themes, binds all of the movements into a single family. You might notice particularly close melodic similarities between the first movement and the Scherzo, and between the second movement and the finale.

Speaking of which, the scene by the brook is an especially remarkable piece, very difficult to conduct owing in part to its layered textures and complex rhythms. It employs full-blown sonata form with an extensive development section and a big coda. All the while it flows along uninterruptedly in a mood of idyllic tranquility, revealing a paradoxical combination of movement and stasis. Once you grasp the form, it seems to get shorter every time you hear it; but the music is so seamless and mellow, and so beautifully euphonious, with the melodies evolving so organically, that at first it can seem to pass by in a blur. The key to following it lies in knowing how the exposition works:

A. First Subject—violins over the "brook music" in the lower strings, immediately repeated by solo woodwinds, leading to a closing theme, or refrain, and coming to a full stop.
B. A tiny bridge or transition in dialogue between violins, horns, and woodwinds (never to be heard again) leads back to the first subject.

This now becomes its own "motion music" as the sound of the brook returns, introducing:

C. Second Subject, on solo bassoon immediately repeated by the violins. This theme is more obviously rhythmic—indeed, it's almost a waltz when played by the full string section. It culminates in the same refrain as previously—I'm almost tempted to call it a musical "picture frame" for the way it borders each initial paragraph.

The development is based mostly on the first subject, and when the main theme returns on the solo flute, babbling brook and all, you know you have arrived at the recapitulation—albeit condensed and subtly recomposed. In the coda, Beethoven does his famous birdsong imitations, and the piece concludes, appropriately, with the refrain. The entire movement, the longest in the symphony, lasts about twelve minutes. If the performance takes much longer, then the brook threatens to stagnate and become a swamp. I've heard versions, unfortunately, that sound more like the *Everglades* Symphony than the *Pastoral*. The music requires great concentration and a keen feeling for musical phrasing and articulation from the players. Some of my favorite performances are those by Arturo Toscanini, George Szell, and Pierre Monteux.

Let's end this chapter, though, by talking about the storm, the most graphic and physical part of the symphony. Indeed, it's so plainly and obviously "what it is" that it seems almost a pity to mention technical matters at all, but doing so briefly can only heighten our enjoyment of the music and increase our wonder at Beethoven's genius. Most of the time, the storm is described and dismissed as a quick introduction to the finale, which it is, of course; but it also has its own distinct form, and it's one that we've encountered before. Basically, the piece has exactly the same shape as one of Beethoven's theatrical overtures: namely, sonata form without a development section.

In this case, the initial soft patter of rain in jagged violin figures represents the first subject. When the storm breaks, we have motion music, appropriately enough. This leads to the second subject in the form of "Beethoven bounce" lightning bolts. After a tiny lull, the first subject returns, followed by substantially varied motion music and then the second subject, now transformed (with screaming piccolo on top) into a swirling vortex of strings and reaching a swift climax of maximum intensity. The rest of the movement consists of a coda that also acts as the transition to the finale, a sonata-rondo (as already mentioned) with one special feature: the main theme of the ritornello, or A section, is varied on each return.

It's remarkable to consider that two works as expressively different as the Fifth and Sixth Symphonies were written in tandem and premiered at the same concert, but it's even more amazing to consider what they have in common. Both works shift the weight of the symphonic argument toward the second half of the work, and both take full advantage of Beethoven's new, gestural language. Although the Fifth may be the most iconic piece of classical music ever written, the Sixth had a more immediate impact on later music, thanks to its programmatic elements. The bottom line is that these two works aren't just landmarks in the history of the symphony, but in the history of music more generally.

Symphonies Nos. 7 and 8

"It's like a lot of yaks jumping about." So said famous British conductor Thomas Beecham when making his excellent recording of Beethoven's Seventh Symphony. Beecham is famous for his wit, but then so is Beethoven, and as a musical description "jumping yaks" sounds like a more colorful version of the "Beethoven bounce." This symphony features some of the best yaks, er . . . bounces . . . around, and uses them as a unifying gesture among and between all of the quick(er) movements. It has some other characteristic gestures as well, which we will discuss in a moment. To start, however, let's consider the Seventh's truly novel handling of the classical orchestra.

As you can see in looking at the orchestration chart at the start of this part of the book, the Seventh requires an orchestra no larger than that of the First and Second Symphonies, or all but one of Haydn's last twelve "London" Symphonies. Once again, for the record, this "standard" ensemble consists of flutes, oboes, clarinets, bassoons, horns, and trumpets in pairs, plus strings and timpani. The power and amplitude that Beethoven gets out of this relatively modest grouping is truly astonishing. He does it in a few ways.

First, as had been increasingly the case throughout the symphonies, he treats the cellos and basses, or collectively the "bass line," with great freedom and flexibility. This is most evident in four places: the first movement's introduction, the start of the second movement Allegretto, and the codas to the first movement and finale, where the bass grinds away with inexorable persistence. By making us listen to the music from the bottom up, as it were, and creating space within the instrumental textures, Beethoven gives the entire ensemble a richness of sonority and impact that you won't find in any earlier music written for similar forces. That's a fact.

Second, the outer movements have those splendid horn parts. These are not just a function of the new openness of sonority just mentioned; they create extraordinary tension and excitement, especially when they get the principal melody. This has precedents—in the first movement of the Sixth Symphony, but even earlier, in one of Haydn's most remarkable symphonies, No. 88 in G major. The difference is that Beethoven previously exploited this special timbre in order to create music of distinctly "pastoral" character. In this symphony, however, he universalizes the sonorous world of the Sixth, making it part of the language of his music more generally.

The third factor that makes the orchestra in this symphony sound so different is Beethoven's treatment of rhythm, and specifically, the rhythmic gesture. Every movement employs to an unprecedented degree the obsessive repetition of tiny rhythmic figures. What prevents monotony is the fact that each of these gestures is distinct, and that they operate at multiple levels in the musical fabric, as elements of both melody and accompaniment. Wagner somewhat misleadingly called this symphony "the apotheosis of the dance," but to the extent that his remark casts light on the music's physicality, its power of movement, he had a valid point.

You can see how Beethoven balances and deploys this emancipated feeling for rhythm over the entire span of the symphony very simply by looking at the time signatures of the various movements:

First Movement
    Introduction (Poco sostenuto): 4/4
    Vivace: 6/8
Second Movement (Allegretto): 4/4
Scherzo (Presto): 3/4
Finale (Allegro con brio): 2/4

As this little outline shows, the music treats the alternation between duple and triple rhythms as a major source of contrast, but also of symmetry, with the two basic kinds of meter appearing alternately, in succession. Commentators often remark on the unusual length and independent form of the first movement introduction (AABAB), but if we look at it in terms of the symphony's large-scale organization, then Beethoven's reason for beginning with a substantial block of music in solid, four-square rhythm becomes clear. Let's move, then, beyond discussion of the symphony's new approach to scoring and sonority and consider the individual movements in greater detail.

As just suggested, the introduction acts as the foundation stone of the entire symphony, not merely as the prelude to the first movement's Vivace. Marked "Poco sostenuto" (a little sustained), which isn't as slow as it's sometimes played, it contains two ideas that relate to the first movement specifically and one that applies to the whole work. The former consist, first, of the four loud chords for full orchestra at the very start, with the space between filled in by a lyrical woodwind melody. This idea is the prototype for what will become the Vivace's first subject, although that's easier to hear at the start of the recapitulation. The second idea that returns later is the introduction's B section, again initially on the woodwinds, and comprising a sort of wavering back and forth (or up and down) between just a few select notes—often in little groups of three—over a narrow range. You will hear something very similar in the first movement's transitional motion music and, above all, in its coda.

These two ideas reveal Beethoven expanding on his technique of binding together otherwise disparate sections through the use of shared musical gestures, this time by exploiting similar melodic shapes. These tunes don't have to be the same, and neither do their rhythms, but the intervals between the notes and, above all, the patterns of repetition create a subtle feeling of similarity that you only start to notice consciously once the music becomes increasingly familiar. Later, romantic composers preferred to repeat entire melodies, perhaps varied, perhaps not, as a unifying force, especially in the form of "motto themes" such as we find, say, at the start of Tchaikovsky's Fourth or Fifth Symphonies, but Beethoven's process is just as effective and even more organic because it respects and maintains the development of an individual movement's proprietary material.

The third idea from the introduction, the one that permeates the whole symphony, appears in the loud repeat of its initial A section, and it couldn't be more primal: musical scales, rising in this case, starting from the lowest notes of the cellos and basses and passing upward through the entire string section. This almost ridiculously simple idea not only establishes the boundaries of the music's expanded soundscape, but it makes every subsequent scale that Beethoven chooses to highlight relate back to its origins at this spot. Other moments where you hear something similar occur:

- in the crisscrossing scales of the first movement development;
- at the climax of the Allegretto's central (B) episode;
- as the principal theme of the Scherzo;
- in the horns at the end of the first subject of the finale;
- at the very end of the symphony. Most of the previous scale-figures had been descending, but in the last movement's explosive coda Beethoven allows them to ascend, as in the introduction, giving the closing bars an extra stamp of finality.

As to the Vivace itself, this is Beethoven's only symphonic movement in monothematic sonata form. You may have heard this term used in connection with Haydn's formal strategies, and as you no doubt can see for yourself, it means "one theme"; but the idea that such a movement employs a single tune as its entire material is very misleading. What it really means is that the music starts developing right away from its initial idea, giving the composer more space to vary and explore it across both the first and second subjects. In fact, it may evolve into quite a few distinct melodies or mottos in the process, which is exactly what happens in the Seventh Symphony. Beethoven's insistence on the omnipresent dactylic rhythm (dum dadum, dum dadum), however, ensures that all of the various ideas sound like the related offspring of the same family.

So powerful is the forward momentum generated by this technique that observing the first movement's exposition repeat turns out to be very problematic. Most modern performances do it as a matter of course, but after the rambunctious appearance of some of Beecham's jumping yaks, the return to the beginning sounds unusually unconvincing. The yaks do a better job introducing the development section, and they return with special hilarity just before the coda (one of them gets amusingly out of step). As already noted, pay particular attention to the cellos and basses in the coda—Beethoven wants you to listen down through the texture and enjoy the process of hearing the source of the music's motoric energy gradually rise to the surface.

The Allegretto second movement instantly became Beethoven's most popular symphonic piece, so much so that contemporary audiences liked to have it stuck into the other symphonies as well to make them more palatable. Given how hard Beethoven worked to ensure that his large works would be perceived as integrated wholes, you can only imagine how galling this practice would have seemed to him. It does say something valuable, however, about contemporary taste and the myth that early audiences for "classical" music were somehow smarter and more sophisticated than modern listeners today. Nonsense.

Although the movement has a very simple form—ABA with coda (BA)—Beethoven's treatment of the music in each section is richly inventive. Initially, section A takes the form of a gently melancholy, minor-key theme scored for violas, divided cellos, and basses, followed by three simple variations in a steady crescendo and diminuendo:

Variation 1: the second violins have the theme, which becomes an accompaniment to a beautiful, sad countermelody for the violas and half of the cellos.
Variation 2: the first violins get the theme, while the second violins play the countermelody. At the repeat of the theme's second half, oboes and bassoon enter, and a big crescendo leads to
Variation 3: Horns and woodwinds have the theme, fortissimo, backed by emphatic beats on the trumpets and timpani. The first violins play the countermelody in their upper register with great passion. Like so much of the music in the first movement, the main melody is built up over multiple repetitions of a simple, basic rhythm, here having a marchlike character.

The central (B) episode consists of a sweetly lyrical, major-key melody, beginning on the clarinet and bassoon and endowed with constantly changing woodwind colors. It culminates in a series of descending and ascending scales that gently recall the music of the introduction. When A returns, Beethoven takes the theme and countermelody and, instead of playing them together, presents them separately, with the countermelody first in the woodwinds. This leads back to the theme on the strings, softly whispered initially as a desolate fugue, but then played once through loudly by the full orchestra. The rest of the movement is coda, starting with a bit of the B melody quickly interrupted by the main theme, its phrases broken up in dialogue between just about everyone in turn, and ultimately leading to the same frosty woodwind chord with which the movement opened.

I want to mention one especially subtle touch in connection with this marvelous piece. It isn't just the opening and final chords, but the transitional passages for woodwinds between the movement's "A" and "B" sections that all are scored for the identical combination of oboes, clarinets, bassoons, and horns. Together, this sonority represents yet another of those gestures that Beethoven increasingly relied on to unify his music and give it, if only subconsciously, that extraordinary feeling of cohesion that later generations came to recognize as the essence of "symphonic" writing.

You very seldom will hear the playful scherzo, with its yak-like opening gesture, presented in the form that Beethoven wrote it. Like the similar movement in the Fourth and Sixth, the scherzo and trio come around twice, but with an ingenious arrangement of repeats. Here is the structure as Beethoven conceived it, keeping in mind that both the scherzo (AB) and the trio (CD) each fall into two halves:

First time: AABBCCDD
Second time: AABCCDD
Third time: AB
Coda: C

As you can see, each time the scherzo returns it loses a sectional repeat and so gets shorter. The first half of the trio, C, has its repeat written out and varied, so it can't be omitted, but the much longer second half repeat can be, and often is. Moreover, in the second go-round Beethoven directs that the repeat of A and most of B be played at a uniformly soft dynamic level.

In short, although the repeats all are pretty much literal, quite a bit of variety is built into the movement. The problem is that, played in full, it's a very long piece—especially if the trio, marked "very much less quick," is taken too slowly. Its theme, supposedly based on a folk song, is as simple as simple can be. Accompanied by a slightly tipsy, burping horn and, at the loud repeat, sustained blasts on the trumpet, the impression it conveys is more than a little grotesque; and although you only hear the whole thing twice (its last appearance in the coda is just a threat that never materializes), many conductors feel that its charms don't sustain the double exposure with all repeats given their due.

Accordingly, interpretations range from no repeats (Karajan's last version), to a strategic selection (most versions), to crudely chopping the movement down to the standard ABA scherzo and trio (Stokowski), to the whole thing as Beethoven left it (Wand and Harnoncourt). Naturally, most period instrument performances play the full version automatically and, unfortunately, tediously. As with all such cases, the success or failure of the interpretation depends very much on how the movement fits within the context of the entire symphony. The Seventh contains no really slow movement, and very little slow music. That makes it very exciting—indeed, probably Beethoven's most exciting symphony overall, but it takes skill to keep the piece from sounding merely frantic. The choices made in this movement constitute a major factor in forming that impression.

The finale is a dynamo; indeed, it is almost machinelike in the way that the inexorable first subject chugs along, thanks to its ingenious construction from interactive rhythmic and melodic components of various shapes and sizes. The very opening gesture might remind you of an automobile engine backfiring a couple of times before starting up. The herd of jumping yaks returns with a vengeance for the second subject, but the exposition's closing idea (one hesitates to call it a theme) is a breakaway whirlwind lashed by vicious runs in the strings. From these elements Beethoven constructs a compact sonata-form structure complete with a full exposition repeat, again often omitted in performance, and possessed of a pulverizing energy unmatched in any symphony before or since. Once again, pay close attention to the cellos and basses in the coda, rumbling along like a freight train that ultimately emerges from a long, dark tunnel into the sunshine of the final bars.

Symphony No. 8

Like the Fifth and Sixth Symphonies, the Seventh and Eighth were conceived as a pair, and like the earlier duo they are as noteworthy for their similarities as for their disparities. The Eighth is Beethoven's shortest symphony. Often it plays for less than twenty-five minutes. Like the Seventh, it has no really slow part, but because Beethoven marks the second movement Allegretto scherzando, the third movement is a minuet and, in fact, the slowest movement in the symphony—a most unusual strategy. If the previous symphony reveals Beethoven at his most expansive in terms of form, with the long first movement introduction and multisectional scherzo, the Eighth is just the opposite. Everything about it is compact, indeed compressed, and this is the quality that gives the music its singular tension. It is a tightly coiled spring of a piece, ready to snap at a moment's notice.

One of the most remarkable aspects of the Eighth is the fact that its scoring has none of that "open" quality so characteristic of the Seventh. The horns do have one very notable solo passage in the trio section of the minuet (with the clarinet), but none for both players in tutti sections of the outer movements, such as we find in the previous work. Woodwinds, too, are used with relative restraint, and mostly for brief periods, injecting washes of color at strategic moments. The real workhorses in this symphony are the strings. Indeed, the violins lead off every single movement with its principal theme. There are no preliminaries and no introductions.

The two symphonies do share one element in Beethoven's handling of the orchestra: the very free and extensive use of the cellos and basses, who often get the tune even in very loud passages, where they can be difficult to hear clearly. Just as in the Seventh, this technique energizes the orchestral texture by creating dueling layers of sonic activity, ratcheting up the tension as the parts jostle against each other for primacy. You shouldn't worry if the bass line isn't always ideally audible. Beethoven wants you to feel the movement as much as hear it. You sense the power down below; and like a whale breaching the ocean surface, the effect is no less thrilling for only becoming visible (or in this case audible) for a moment before sinking back into the depths.

The first movement, which goes off like a shot, is either very loud or very soft, mostly the former. Its sonata-form structure is preternaturally clear, with four distinct ideas parceled out over the course of the exposition: the first subject in dialogue between the full orchestra and quiet woodwinds, driving transitional "motion music"; a gentler second subject for violins, then woodwinds; and a closing theme for jumping yaks alternating with quiet rejoinders from woodwinds and strings. It all culminates in a vivacious "Beethoven bounce." Notice that all of these ideas (except for the motion music) are dialogues, and no one has a true solo. The general impression we get is of one big paragraph for the whole orchestra in full cry.

Because the movement is relatively short, the exposition repeat is almost always observed; unlike in the Seventh, Beethoven has clearly designed the music to encourage the players to take it. The development section is amazing. Although it begins quietly with a four-note, repeated gesture in the violas, then cellos, it very quickly works up a huge head of steam, starting with a fugal episode based on the first subject, and then driving at full volume and power to the most exciting moment of recapitulation in all of the symphonies. This is one of those places where you have to pay attention to the bass line, if you can hear it, because it has the tune. The whole passage, with its unbearable tension, rises to a shattering climax, and I do use the word *climax* pointedly, if you know what I mean. Trust me: it's very graphic.

On the other side of this musical summit, the recapitulation is mostly regular, although the loud transition theme is recast as a more lyrical melody on the violins. It also has a marvelous, very substantial "coda that just won't quit." The music repeatedly tries to find a triumphant ending but finally gives up and, surprisingly, settles for the symphony's opening bar, played softly. In this moment we realize that Beethoven's Eighth is not only his shortest symphony but also his funniest, and like all of the best humor, its brevity only enhances its wit.

The delicious Allegretto scherzando has been described as either a humorous imitation of Mälzel's newly invented metronome, an homage to Haydn's famous *Clock* Symphony (no. 101), or a little bit of both. To be frank, neither of these comparisons is particularly helpful because it shifts the focus to the repeated-chord accompaniment in the winds, whereas the entire point of the movement is the delightfully droll extended dialogue between the violins and basses. The entire piece plays for only about three and a half minutes, and its form, believe it or not, is the same as that of the thunderstorm in the Sixth Symphony—namely, the sort of sonata without development typical of Beethoven's theatrical overtures. Given the movement's tiny size, its coda is surprisingly large, once again very funny, with the ending the same shocking "Bronx cheer" (or perhaps it's a dog shaking itself dry after a bath) that we first heard at the end of the second subject.

Beethoven's designation of the third movement is "Tempo di menuetto." Is there a difference between this and a plain minuet? Formally, no, but expressively, perhaps. Many commentators suggest that the minuet was "obsolete" at the time that the symphony was composed in 1812. This isn't true. First of all, stylized dance forms such as symphonic minuets don't go out of fashion. The very idea is fundamentally meaningless. Mendelssohn was writing a modern one a couple of decades later in his *Italian* Symphony, and no one thought anything of it. The music remains as current as its last artful use, wherever and whenever that happens.

Second, what Beethoven has in fact composed is a deliberately old-fashioned minuet in aristocratic style—a lumbering, pompous, exaggerated movement that is as much "about" the old minuet as it is a legitimate exemplar of the form. In other words, the music's obsolescence is entirely deliberate. It's not too surprising, under the circumstances, that most commentators then and now have missed the joke; but comical the music certainly is nonetheless, particularly at the end of the A section when the parts sound a bit out of sync and the timpani starts pounding futilely to bring everyone back in line.

As previously mentioned, the trio section features the horns and clarinet over a triplet accompaniment in the cellos. It is the only extended solo in the entire symphony, and this alone gives the music a curiously nostalgic quality. Heard in context, it reminds us more strongly than any other single moment that the Eighth is a composition for the whole orchestra almost throughout, and that Beethoven's scoring is no less revolutionary in its radically compressed and kaleidoscopic way than was his treatment of the ensemble in the Seventh. Anyway, if you find the minuet too clunky for your taste, check out the opening of the finale, which starts with what sounds suspiciously like a sleek, flashy, modernized version of the same tune.

I mentioned the finale back in chapter 1 as perhaps the finest example of the "coda that just won't quit" in all of Beethoven, because it occupies almost exactly half of the movement. Another brilliant essay in sonata form (this time without a repeat), it's also worth pointing out that the development section features an extensive contrapuntal episode, just as happened in the first movement. Yet again, we hear Beethoven playing with musical gestures (in this case, a texture) as a means of creating unity without having to quote prior themes or motives to get across his point. It's another instance of his very sophisticated compositional technique—sophisticated not in the sense of being excessively complex but, rather, in having a keen sense of balance and proportion in order to give each moment a feeling of inevitable rightness.

I need to mention one other example of this quality. At the start of the finale, right after the pianissimo announcement of the principal theme in the violins, the orchestra blasts out a sudden, obviously foreign note. It seems to come out of nowhere, but it will play a big role in the coda, where it goes to war against the rest of the orchestra and kicks the theme into a panicked, minor key. It's worth comparing this procedure to the similar moment at the start of the *Eroica* Symphony, where the exact same note, C-sharp coincidentally, is supposed to strike us as a big deal in the coda of that movement, some twelve minutes later. As I mentioned, the significance of that event is debatable, but it certainly isn't here; and I can't help but think that because Beethoven takes extra pains to make sure that we know a big deal when we hear one, this example offers telling evidence of the way in which he's refined his compositional technique in the ensuing years. Again, greater sophistication doesn't mean greater complexity but, rather, greater clarity of expression.

Despite being an unalloyed delight from first note to last, Beethoven's Eighth is, along with the Fourth, his least popular symphony. Its brevity and humorous tone often are mistaken for shallowness, luring conductors to treat it condescendingly, with kid gloves, in performance. The truth, as I hope I've convinced you, is just the opposite. Our perception of musical "depth" should not be limited to music that's self-evidently ambitious, or long, or complicated, or miserable. In the hands of conductors such as Toscanini, Scherchen, or the more recent Haitink, artists who are willing to seize the music and give it a good shake, the result has a concentrated power every bit as compelling as anything in Beethoven's grander works.

Wellington's Victory (*aka* Battle Symphony)

Yes, *Wellington's Victory* has a whole chapter to itself, but don't worry, it will be a short one. Like the *Pastoral* Symphony, this is another piece that has been dogged by Beethoven's own words about it. When a contemporary critic blasted the work as a piece of trash, Beethoven responded, "What I shit is better than his loftiest thoughts." And so the idea that Beethoven deemed the piece "shit" has persisted ever since. Certainly, *Wellington's Victory* is a potboiler, an occasional work, but comparing it to excrement strikes me as a bit harsh. Besides—and this is the reason it has a chapter to itself—for no other work did Beethoven take more pains to give detailed performance instructions. In short, he *cared*, deeply, about ensuring that it made the proper effect and received the best possible execution.

For the record, the victory being celebrated is the English triumph over the French at the Battle of Vitoria during the Napoleonic Wars. In 1813, joint British, Spanish, and Portuguese forces under Wellington defeated the French armies in Spain and freed the Spanish Peninsula from Napoleonic domination. Beethoven wrote three versions of his battle piece, including one for Johann Mälzel's Panharmonicon, a mechanical orchestra that he showed off in tours around Europe. The growing success of the work induced Beethoven to arrange the final score that we hear today; so, again, we see that he took great pains over it. Remember, Mayr's funeral cantata in Beethoven's memory quotes from it, evidence of just how popular the music became.

This is how the music, which plays for about fifteen minutes, proceeds:

Part One:

1. Drums followed by a trumpet fanfare announcing the approach of the English army.
2. The orchestra plays an English march—"Rule Britannia."
3. Drum followed by a trumpet fanfare announcing the approach of the French army.
4. The orchestra plays a French march—"Marlborough," or "For He's a Jolly Good Fellow," as it's known today.
5. The French trumpets issue a challenge, and English trumpets reply with a counterchallenge.
6. The battle begins. Beethoven marks opposing English and French cannon shots in the score with extreme precision, and uses rachets (cog rattles) to imitate musket fire. In modern recordings, real gunfire often is dubbed in. The entry of the snare drums signals the charging armies, and the fighting reaches a fearsome climax in which the English defeat the French. A soft, minor-key version of "Marlborough" signals their dejected retreat as isolated cannon shots pursue them.

Part Two: Victory Symphony

This celebratory movement is a kind of rondo in which the victory music enfolds two statements of "God Save the King" in slower tempo. The course of the music is otherwise self-explanatory, and at the very end the bass drum, cymbals, and triangle add to the festivities exactly as they will at the conclusion of the Ninth Symphony.

Beethoven's preface to the score is a remarkable document, well worth reading for what it tells us about the piece as well as contemporary performance practice. I quote it in full, from the orchestral score published by Dover Editions, with my own adjustments to the German translation. The Dover score, by the way, is nicely printed and quite inexpensive, so if you want to take the plunge, by all means go ahead.

Beethoven's Instructions for Performing *Wellington's Victory*

1. Two different wind and brass bands must be used. The first band plays the first march, Rule Britannia (the English); the second band plays the second march, Marlborough (the French). In the later movements, both bands play together. The rest of the orchestra should naturally be as large as possible proportionally; the bigger the hall, the larger the ensemble.

2. The two bass drums (not large Turkish drums) that imitate cannon shots should be the largest size possible (here they measured 5 Viennese feet in diameter). This is the size used in theaters to imitate thunder (the true Turkish drum is used solely in the orchestra). They must be placed away from the orchestra, on opposite sides, one representing the English army, and the other the French. This should be arranged as the hall permits, but neither should be visible to the audience. The conductor who beats time for both forces may, of course, stand in front. The players in charge of the cannon shots must not in any event be right in the orchestra, but rather placed at a reasonable distance, and these devices must be played by very good musicians. (Here in Vienna they were played by respected conductors).

3. The devices called ratchets (rattles), which represented musket fire and are usually used in theaters for thunder crashes, as well as for army musket fire too, must also be placed on opposite sides, close to the cannons. Specific indications are given for these, but the parts should nonetheless be given to players with good sense and taste [Note: Yeah, right!]. The only condition is that they should never come in at the start of a new tempo, except in the Presto: Alla breve, so that the theme of each section can be clearly heard. In the "Charge" movement they don't play at all.

4. The trumpets in E-flat and C are also played on opposing sides, close to the artillery—those in E-flat on the English side, and those in C on the French side. Additionally, four trumpets play in the orchestra, of which the two trumpets in E-flat and C must then be played standing in the orchestra [Note: Musicians in those days at orchestral concerts mostly played standing].

5. Additionally, there must be two standard snare drums on each side; these players perform a sort of introduction on their drums before each march. Note, however, that these introductions shouldn't last too long, though longer than the printed music indicates; and wherever possible they should start in the far distance and move closer and closer in order to imitate the advancing armies in as realistic a manner as possible.

6. Regarding the tempos, the following instructions should be kept in mind:

1) The English march not too fast; the French march a bit livelier. The first tempo after the French march: moderato; the second subsequent 3/8 slightly slower. In the "Charge" it would be a good idea to steadily increase the tempo. The final tempo, 6/8 andante, not too fast.

2) In the Victory Symphony, the introduction not too fast, the second tempo, C [Note: That is, common time or 4/4], very lively. The final tempo, 3/8, not too fast, almost allegretto. Where there is an indication that only two 1st violins, two 2nd violins, two violas and two cellos should play, in a larger hall it's acceptable for three or four of each to play, but with the best performers on each part.

7. It is very necessary in the orchestral performance that, in addition to the concertmaster, a conductor must beat time for the whole ensemble. Both of them need to keep the overall effect in mind at every point, so that the instrumental music isn't drowned out by the rattles, drums, and other contraptions. Generally speaking, the proportions of the hall, the size of the orchestra, and the ratio of these factors should govern the manner of conducting.

8. In the Victory Symphony there are also two wind and brass bands, but the second band does not play in piano [Note: Quiet] or solo passages.

Vienna, December 1815
—Ludwig van Beethoven

Finally, it's worth remembering that in his lifetime Beethoven had a reputation as a "difficult" composer: modern, uncompromising, writing works of deliberate and intimidating complexity. Even the music of the early and charming *Prometheus* ballet was considered too "learned." His last string quartets were seen as incomprehensible, even by many of his admirers. *Wellington's Victory* is a "pops" piece, intended for general consumption. That it worked so well should not be seen as a lapse in standards but, rather, as a tribute to Beethoven's professionalism and willingness to give his audience a quarter hour of unchallenging, unabashed fun. There is no reason why we shouldn't enjoy it accordingly.

Symphony No. 9 (Choral)

Ten years passed between Beethoven's Eighth and Ninth Symphonies. In the interim, his deafness became complete, his life grew progressively more miserable, and his music became ever more personal and difficult to pigeonhole. The Ninth and its companion work, the Missa Solemnis, represent Beethoven's (surely unintended) farewell to both the orchestra and the voice, as well as an apotheosis of his art and musical philosophy. The symphony, especially, despite reservations occasionally aimed at the choral finale, entered the repertoire almost immediately as one of the pinnacles of Western culture and has remained there ever since.

The message of the Ninth Symphony requires no explanation. It's all there in the text of the finale, and all you have to do is look at the words and enjoy Beethoven's setting of them. The three big instrumental movements that come first reveal different emotional states on the way to that final resolution. So much ink has been spilled describing and analyzing them that it's tempting to surrender to the inevitable and say, "Just go listen to it," and leave it at that. However, I do have some observations consistent with the discussion of the previous symphonies that will provide points of entry into the music's original and highly distinctive sound world, and I propose to focus on them accordingly.

A myth surrounds large works: because they are bigger, their forms and expressive ends must necessarily be more complicated. This isn't true. To a remarkable degree, large forms often are simpler than smaller ones in many respects, because the more time and attention you have to spend listening, the more obvious and memorable the major signposts have to be to lodge in your memory and make the argument comprehensible. No piece of music demonstrates this rule more clearly than Beethoven's Ninth. It takes Beethoven's gestural language to an entirely new level of simplicity and effectiveness, while at the same time using this to highlight new elements of his expressive language.

In his late works, beginning with the *Hammerklavier* Sonata for piano of about 1818, Beethoven became fascinated with the contrast between dramatic and rhetorical musical expression. I mentioned this briefly in considering *The Consecration of the House* Overture. The dramatic side, which he had long ago mastered more potently than any of his predecessors is embodied in the sonata style. Rhetorical music, for Beethoven, came in two forms, both of which represent a kind of musical discussion—the power of passionate language and debate as opposed to the power of dynamic activity. These forms were the fugue, a type of counterpoint in which several voices discuss a given subject, both in turn and simultaneously; and variations, a series of comments or elaborations on a given theme.

Beethoven already had used both of these rhetorical devices many times previously, often together, such as the fugues in the variation finale of the *Eroica* Symphony. The second movement of the Fifth Symphony is a kind of variation form, while you will recall the fugato at the start of the First Symphony's slow movement. All of these previous recourses to rhetoric, however, remain subservient to the overriding sonata style. In later works, however, such as we saw in *The Consecration of the House* Overture, Beethoven places the rhetorical style on equal footing. His intent seems to have been to increase the music's expressive force by considering his material from both perspectives simultaneously.

The Ninth Symphony reveals him doing this especially effectively. It begins with two movements in sonata form, both of which include fugues, and ends with two movements in variation form, the last highly dramatic in its range of incident. The two kinds of music operate in partnership to put across Beethoven's expressive point; and the purely verbal idea that "all men are brothers," announced in the finale, finds its analog in the purely music process that affirms dramatic and rhetorical expression as joint partners in a shared goal.

The musical argument proceeds in stages, with sonata elements gradually yielding to rhetorical ones, movement by movement. In the opening Allegro ma non troppo un poco maestoso [Quickly, not too much, a bit majestically], drama reigns in the form of a gripping, minor-key sonata form without exposition repeat. The music marches forward with inexorable purpose, its first subject swiftly evolving out of a mysterious harmonic void into a descending unison theme of tremendous power.

Two gestural elements require your special attention, one short term, and the other long term. The short-term element is the first subject's second phrase, containing eight notes in an emphatic jagged rhythm. This brief motive will become the source of much of the ensuing activity, including the subject of the big fugue in the middle of the development section—the music's major point of rhetorical emphasis.

The long-term element is simplicity itself and the first potentially melodic thing you hear: a figure of two descending notes, usually the first shorter than the second (da-dum). Each of the symphony's first three movements begins with this gesture, repeated several times as a sort of prelude. It then functions thematically, as the starting point of all of the principal tunes (both of them in the Adagio). Throughout the first movement, Beethoven drives home the importance of this tiny idea, nowhere more so than at the start of the recapitulation, where trumpets and timpani hammer it into our brains with terrifying force.

The gesture also leads off Beethoven's grandest and grimmest "coda that just won't quit," at first softly but very persistently, then returning at the end with increasingly ferocious power. In the Scherzo it becomes a "Beethoven bounce" and the principal source of motive energy, repeated obsessively almost to the point of lunacy. The Adagio gives it to the bassoons and clarinets in the very first bars. It even turns up in the finale to introduce the concluding choral celebration, as a reminder of just how far we've come.

Given the music's melodic and emotional richness, it's easy to dismiss points such as this as naive and simplistic, but I continue to believe that the greatest composers usually place all of the information you need to enjoy and understand their works on the surface, in plain sight. The craft needs to be there, too, at the level of deep structure, but you don't need to know how to build a house in order to live in one, and too many discussions of Beethoven's music focus on questions of the infrastructure buried in the walls at the expense of the magnificent and impactful interior designs. And let's not kid ourselves. It's kind of hard to get a thrill from plumbing and electrical wiring, whereas those mahogany finishes and marble countertops will seal the deal every time.

Beethoven's handling of the orchestra in the Ninth definitely belongs in the "mahogany finishes" category. It presents many problems of balance that require adjustment in performance, but the basic concept always is clear. Like the Eighth Symphony—but, of course, on a much larger scale—the Ninth is a composition for the whole orchestra, almost all of the time. This doesn't mean it lacks instrumental solos, especially for horn and oboe in the trio of the Scherzo, or the famous lick for fourth horn in the Adagio, but these are rare. For the most part, Beethoven's scoring offers a kaleidoscope of constantly shifting colors. He treats the woodwinds, especially, as an independent unit virtually equivalent to the strings, featuring them in small groups tossing bits of melody back and forth while maintaining a seamless, lyrical line.

You can hear this very clearly in a few especially significant spots. First, in the second subject in the first movement, where strings and winds collaborate to create melodic paragraphs of striking breadth and variety before the full orchestra gathers itself to bring the exposition to a close with a typical Beethoven bounce (by now the yaks have long returned to Mongolia). Another iconic moment featuring this new handling of the woodwind section occurs in the Adagio, where the main melody is played by the violins, with woodwinds echoing each phrase. Later, the theme is varied in the strings, but the woodwind echoes remain unchanged, keeping the original melody firmly in view even as its variation passes before us. It's an especially wonderful example of "whole orchestra" scoring, and it gives the music an unforgettably expressive fullness of tone.

The Scherzo's A section also features a remarkable degree of interplay between strings and woodwinds. It employs full sonata form but has the typical scherzo shape with two halves, both repeated. The first half contains the exposition, with the first subject a fugato for strings and a second subject for woodwinds accompanied by the symphony's descending, motto gesture. The second half includes the development (woodwinds lead, with those famous solo timpani interruptions); the very violent recapitulation of the first subject in the full orchestra; and the second subject for woodwinds, as before. An accelerating codetta leads to the trio (or B section), featuring a childlike melody initially for solo horn and oboe in counterpoint, then a warm answer from the strings, with the first entrance of the trombones at the climaxes.

When the Scherzo returns, it loses its repeats, at least in the latest critical edition. Some performances nonetheless include all of them after the trio. This makes the movement extremely long, even though the full A section only comes back once. As in all such cases, the choice is up to the conductor, both here and with respect to repeats the first time around. Beethoven does pretend that he wants the trio to return one last time, but the orchestra interjects with an emphatic closing gesture. The real reason we don't hear the full scherzo-trio complex all over again, of course, is that the main body of the movement already uses an expansive example of sonata form. In other words, it is complete after the first time through, so there really isn't room or reason for another go-round.

The Adagio is a set of variations on two alternating but related themes, the second more flowing than the first. Both are serene and absolutely gorgeous. Beethoven has designed this movement to exploit a marvelous formal ambiguity. Because he has two distinct themes, we have no way of knowing, when we first hear them, that we are not listening to the first and second subjects of yet another movement in sonata form. Even the first theme's initial variation could be either the start of the development section or perhaps the recapitulation in a typical sonata-without-development slow movement. It's only when the variation of the second theme arrives that we realize that we've very gently and imperceptibly moved beyond the sonata style into another expressive realm entirely.

This shift in emphasis from the dramatic to the rhetorical, from action to contemplation, comprises perhaps the most momentous event in the entire symphony. It not only serves the music's immediate expressive purpose of providing an oasis of spiritual tranquility, but it quietly sets up Beethoven's ultimate rhetorical stroke: the introduction of voices in the finale, thereby fulfilling the symphonic dictum that the music should never consist of effects without causes. Nothing happens without purpose or justification. The Adagio also offers us a telling lesson worth keeping in mind: specifically, that major musical signposts need not necessarily occur at the loudest or most obvious points.

Beethoven provides just as many variations as he needs to accomplish this larger goal: two versions of the first theme, each becoming swifter as the result of being more elaborately ornamented and filigreed, and only one variation of the second theme. This still makes for a very spacious movement at the slow basic tempo. There is also one free episode, mainly for the woodwinds and based on the first theme (culminating in that famous solo for fourth horn). The second and most intricate variation of the principal theme, which follows immediately on the episode, leads to a vigorous fanfare figure for the full orchestra, including trumpets and timpani. At first the variation takes no notice of this interjection and continues on, unruffled, until the fanfare returns again, this time more insistently and leading to a thrilling change of key.

Its job of variations now finished, the remainder of the movement is coda—a lot of coda—so the form isn't strict at all. Just the opposite. You get a feeling of progressively increasing, rhapsodic freedom—of an ecstatic meditation that never wants to end. Aside from the fanfare, which constitutes the movement's single dramatic stroke, Beethoven doesn't let anything interrupt what we now recognize as the music's intensely lyrical, sublime rhetoric.

The finale is another set of free variations. As already suggested, the last movement of the *Eroica* Symphony provides the precedent for it, with a set of variations containing two fugues along the way, just as Beethoven will do here. That earlier finale even starts similarly, with a loud commotion, and then goes through a kind of process of discovery in search of its principal theme. Beethoven's solution to the analogous situation in the Ninth, however, is quite different and wholly unique.

It begins with what the Germans memorably call a "Schreckensfanfare," or "horror fanfare." This is yet another of those "time-to-wake-up" gestures that Beethoven loves to use to counter a prolonged period of peace and quiet. After this dissonant hubbub, the cellos and basses play a recitative in which they actively search for the theme of finale, rejecting in turn all of the previous tunes. Beethoven originally wrote words for these recitatives, and when he had what he wanted, he simply dropped the text and left the

Symphony No. 9 (Choral)

music intact. The result is as close to human speech as instruments ever have come and a rhetorical statement of the highest order.

This passage of instrumental recitative also reveals the importance of that tiny, two-note motto gesture, for it contains the first and only time that we hear all of the symphony's main themes played one after the other, in close succession, and summarily dismissed. In this context, their resemblance becomes plainly audible. By rejecting them, the cellos and basses seem to be saying, "You see, it's just the same old stuff over and over again. We need something totally new."

Finally, the lower strings "discover" the finale's famous joy theme. It is completely new, especially because it does not share the motto gesture. The orchestra alone then plays it in three simple variations with the full ensemble gradually joining in—much as happens in the Allegretto of the Seventh Symphony. But mere instruments aren't enough to get across the music's point. The horror fanfare returns, and along with it the original recitative to Beethoven's words, now sung by the baritone soloist (I follow each German stanza with my own inimitable translation of the bits of Schiller's "Ode to Joy" that Beethoven set):

Baritone recitative (words by Beethoven):

> O Freunde, nicht diese Töne!
> Sondern laßt uns angenehmere anstimmen,
> und freudenvollere.
>
> *Oh friends, not these sounds! Rather, let us tune our voices more pleasingly and joyfully.*

Then the baritone and chorus sing the joy theme to the words that Beethoven always planned that it should express.

Baritone and chorus (words by Schiller):

> Freude, schöner Götterfunken,
> Tochter aus Elysium!
> wir betreten feuertrunken,
> himmlische, Dein Heiligtum.
> Deine Zauber binden wieder,
> was die Mode streng geteilt,
> alle Menschen werden Brüder,
> wo Dein sanfter Flügel weilt.

> *Joy, beautiful god-sparked daughter of Elysium! We approach your heavenly sanctuary drunk with fire. Your magic reunites what convention sternly divided, and all men become brothers where your gentle wings overspread.*

The next two variations are set for the quartet of soloists and the chorus. They grow increasingly elaborate. The solo vocal lines are famously all but impossible and require four truly stellar singers.

Solo quartet and chorus:

> Wem der große Wurf gelungen,
> eines Freundes Freund zu sein,
> wer ein holdes Weib errungen,
> mische seinen Jubel ein!
> Ja, wer auch nur eine Seele
> sein nennt auf dem Erdenrund!
> Und wer's nie gekonnt, der stehle
> weinend sich aus diesem Bund!

> *Whoever has had the great fortune to be a friend's friend; he who has found a loving wife, let him join our jubilation—yes—anyone on this earth who claims a soul as his own; and he who cannot let him depart crying from our association.*

> Freude trinken alle Wesen
> an den Brüsten der Natur;
> alle Guten, alle Bösen
> folgen ihrer Rosenspur.
> Küsse gab sie uns und Reben,
> einen Freund, geprüft im Tod;
> wollust ward dem Wurm gegeben,
> und der Cherub steht vor Gott.

> *All beings drink in joy at nature's breast. The good and bad alike follow her path of roses. Kisses and wine she gives us, even unto death. Even the worm was given desire, and the angel stands before God.*

The words "before God" lead to a huge choral climax almost identical to the one on the word "Kraft" (strength or power) in the Choral Fantasy, only longer and louder. As he so often does in the Missa Solemnis, Beethoven contrasts the overwhelming glory of God's majesty to the puny insignificance of man. The choral shout cuts off abruptly as grotesque, low burps from the contrabassoon and bass drum initiate a march variation on the joy theme, including cymbals and triangle, and sung by the tenor backed by the male chorus.

Tenor and male chorus:

> Froh, wie seine Sonnen fliegen
> durch des Himmels prächt'gen Plan,
> laufet, Brüder, eure Bahn,
> freudig, wie ein Held zum Siegen.
>
> *Happily, as the sun flies according to heaven's magnificent design, run brothers along your route joyfully, like a victorious hero.*

The march overflows into an orchestral variation comprising the first of the movement's two fugues. Both are, in fact, double fugues—that is, they feature two themes presented in quick succession. The second theme in this case is a variant of the actual joy tune while the first adopts the rhythm of the preceding march. Once the fugue has run its course, the full chorus offers a boisterous reprise of the first stanza with the melody in its original form; but with joy now well and truly established as the subject of the musical discourse, Beethoven interrupts the flow of the variations for an independent episode. The tenors and basses of the chorus sternly proclaim the following text accompanied by the trombones, and the full choir answers after each pair of lines. The mood becomes hushed and solemn at the words "Do you bow down, millions?" and then mysterious and "spacey" at the idea of God dwelling beyond the stars.

Chorus:

> Seid umschlungen, Millionen!
> diesen Kuß der ganzen Welt!
> Brüder, über'm Sternenzelt
> muß ein lieber Vater wohnen!
>
> *Be embraced, millions! This kiss is for the whole world. Brothers, beyond the field of stars a loving Father must dwell.*

> Ihr stürzt nieder, Millionen?
> Ahnest du den Schöpfer, Welt?
> Such' ihn über'm Sternenzelt!
> Über Sternen muß er wohnen.
>
> *Do you bow down, millions? Do you feel the Creator, world? Search beyond the field of stars. Beyond the stars He must dwell.*

The remainder of the movement consists of two additional variations based on repetition of the words above. Immediately following the "space music," the choir begins another exuberant double fugue that combines the joy theme (and text) with the "Be embraced" music. This fugue is legendary for its hair-raising climax in which the sopranos have to hold a high A for what seems (to them) like weeks on end. The fugue dissolves into further contemplation of God dwelling beyond the stars, leading at last to the final variation. This is a childlike round initiated by the soloists and based on the first stanza of the poem. The very embodiment of innocent fun, we hear it twice before the soloists interrupt with an extended cadenza on the same text. This must be conducted at a flowing tempo in order to keep the singers from dying of oxygen deprivation and the audience from plugging its ears in distress.

Suddenly, the orchestra reminds us of the symphony's descending, two-note motto for a last time, and in a flash the entire vocal and orchestral apparatus, with percussion going nuts, comes alive in a coda that starts with the "Be embraced" music in quicker tempo. The final word, however, goes to one last apotheosis of "God-sparked joy" as the full orchestra races away Prestissimo and thrillingly carries the music right up into the heavens. It's worth noting that Beethoven's metronome markings in these closing pages really do work against both his verbal instructions and the expressive intent of the music. Wilhelm Furtwängler was notably famous for taking Beethoven himself, but not his metronome, at his word and playing the final Prestissimo as fast as humanly possible—sometimes even faster. Whether or not it always worked, he surely got the point far better than the "historically informed" purists.

No matter how they're done, if the closing bars don't raise the roof, then something isn't right. Fortunately, most conductors do recognize the Ninth Symphony as something special and save their best efforts for it. Given the music's length and difficulty in performance, not to mention the potential for disaster, it's remarkable that so many excellent recordings exist. The list included in the discography provides a generous selection of widely differing interpretations that should keep you listening to this inimitable masterpiece for many, many years to come.

To close this discussion of the Ninth Symphony, let me return briefly to the contrast between Beethoven's "dramatic" and "rhetorical" styles.

Symphony No. 9 (Choral)

These concepts can appear confusing at first, but the crucial thing to realize is that the distinction is not a question of what the music expresses, but rather how it gets us there. In the more goal-oriented, dramatic sonata style, at least as Beethoven handles it, the music develops continuously to the end. Although there will undoubtedly be many surprises along the way—not the least in those marvelous "codas that just won't quit"—the feeling of forward momentum is very much a part of the listening experience. The rhetorical style, on the other hand, takes time to highlight the many interesting and colorful stops along the journey (in the form of variations), or to pause and discuss their significance (in the fugues).

In the Ninth, the expressive point of the finale, specifically the feeling of "joy," arrives early on, with the discovery of the famous tune that will shortly acquire actual words. The rest of the movement explores this basic concept from different perspectives, both vocal and purely instrumental. The music is no less highly contrasted, brilliant, or impactful as a result. I mean, can anything sound more exciting than the movement's great choral fugue, or its raucous closing pages? Rather, its form gives Beethoven the opportunity to treat a single, overriding idea at greater length than a more dramatic presentation normally offers. In short, we can feel the impact of joy as a function of its conflict with some other contrasting emotions, or we can experience joy, joy, and more joy, all by itself in all of its different manifestations.

This is the shift in focus that Beethoven achieves as the Ninth Symphony proceeds. He wants to use every technique at his disposal to give his music the maximum expressive force. Accordingly, after a symphonic journey in the first three movements of unprecedented length and richness, an especially emphatic rhetorical statement provides the most fitting finale possible. Beethoven's contemporaries, who had far less of a sense of big, multi-movement musical works as organic wholes than we do today, certainly didn't get the point, and the subtleties of his method may not be something that you recognize right away at a first encounter. However, trust me when I say that you will hear them inevitably and instinctively respond to them nonetheless, because they combine to make this iconic work a musical experience unlike any other.

Conclusion
The Quasi-Orchestral Beethoven

Septet in E-flat Major, op. 20
String Quartet no. 11 in F Minor, op. 95 (*Serioso*)
Piano Sonata no. 29 in B-flat Major, op. 106
   (*Hammerklavier*)
Late String Quartets, op. 127, 130–32, 135
Große Fuge, op. 133

Discography

NBC Symphony Orchestra/Arturo Toscanini (Septet and
   String Quartet, op. 135 [middle movements only])
Royal Philharmonic Orchestra/Felix Weingartner
Vienna Philharmonic/Leonard Bernstein (String Quartets,
   op. 131 and 135)
Vienna Philharmonic/André Previn (String Quartet, op. 131
   + Verdi: Quartet)
Concertgebouw Chamber Orchestra/Marco Bono (String
   Quartet, op. 95 + Schubert: Quartet no. 14 *Death and
   the Maiden*)
C. P. E. Bach Chamber Orchestra/Hartmut Haenchen (String
   Quartet, op. 95 + Schubert: Quartet no. 14 *Death and
   the Maiden*)

Moscow Soloists/Yuri Bashmet (String Quartet, op. 95 +
   Schubert: Quartet no. 14 *Death and the Maiden*)
Vienna Philharmonic/Christoph von Dohnányi (String
   Quartet, op. 95 + Brahms: Piano Quartet no. 1)
Philharmonia Orchestra/Otto Klemperer (Große Fuge)
Camerata Nordica/Terje Tønnesen (Late String Quartets incl.
   Große Fuge)

If you believe that Beethoven didn't write enough orchestral music, then this conclusion offers just the ticket. We live at a time when performers are desperate to make a name for themselves by finding proprietary repertoire—but not just any proprietary repertoire. I'm talking about unknown works by great composers. This is a tall order in the best of circumstances, and no one is more "known" than Beethoven. Had he been a lesser light, like England's Edward Elgar, for example, some enterprising modern composer wanting to make a name for himself would take a few incomplete sketches, put them together in a vaguely idiomatic way, and call the result "Symphony no. 3."

That really happened. The classical music world is full of pieces that famous dead composers never wrote. All they had to do was think about it and jot down a few scribbles and an army of nobodies, led by their publishers and a flotilla of public relations people, will do the rest. Beethoven's alleged "Tenth Symphony" is one such piece. It surfaces now and again, but it has never caught on. Here, it would seem, is a composer whose reputation is simply too exalted to mess with.

Well, maybe not quite. Consider another solution, one that gives performers something "new" by Beethoven that doesn't necessarily disgrace his name: the orchestral transcription.

As noted at the beginning of this book, Beethoven's music, even his chamber music, has an inherent size and conceptual grandeur that make it uniquely suited to the orchestral medium. He really did it to himself, truth be told, starting with the Große Fuge (Grand Fugue) for string quartet. This originally was the finale to op. 130, but he later detached it when the players found the music too difficult. Contemporary audiences also hated it. Although many quartets today restore Beethoven's original intentions, the Große Fuge remains a big, long (more than fifteen minutes), deliberately ugly but ultimately transcendental beast of a piece that arguably loses nothing and gains much when transferred to the medium of string orchestra. At least, surprisingly few experts have complained about the practice. It seems that larger forces allow for a greater focus on the music itself, as distinct from the sheer gnarliness of the writing and the really appalling difficulties of execution.

From the Große Fuge, it was only a matter of time before conductors and arrangers got their hands on the remaining late quartets, works that regularly are described as "too big" for the chamber music medium. All of them have been arranged for string orchestra, and the truth is that they work very well that way even if purists may kvetch. But then, purists always kvetch. Quite a few magnificent performances are available, with more appearing all the time, and I list some of the best of them in the discography. The most famous such transcription is Gustav Mahler's arrangement of the *Serioso* Quartet, op. 95. When one great composer lavishes his attention on an illustrious predecessor, the results often have an aesthetic interest above and apart from questions of idiomatic style. As it turns out, Mahler's recasting is a model of sensitivity. It usually comes coupled to the same composer's similar arrangement of Schubert's *Death and the Maiden* Quartet.

Leonard Bernstein regarded his recordings of two Beethoven string quartets with the Vienna Philharmonic as the best things he ever did with that orchestra, which is saying a lot. I'd also like to give a shout-out to Terja Tønnesen's arrangements of all of the late quartets for the Camerata Nordica—tasteful, intelligent, and stunningly well played by a crack group of superb strings. Beethoven's late quartets are challenging but extraordinary works, so if hearing them in their orchestral guise helps them go down better, then I'm all for it.

The other Beethoven arrangements listed are more hit-and-miss. The early Septet, a delightful suite in six movements originally scored for clarinet, horn, bassoon, violin, viola, cello, and double bass, is already quasi-orchestral in layout. Sometimes it's performed with a conductor in charge. It works beautifully with a few extra strings, as Toscanini's recording proves. The *Hammerklavier* Sonata, on the other hand, is piano music from start to finish. Conductor Felix Weingartner was a

Beethoven specialist, but his arrangement of the sonata for full orchestra sounds grotesque, and he should have known better. Leaving aside the very limited historical recording, none of it works.

As this book goes to press, we are celebrating the 250th anniversary of Beethoven's birth. Dozens of new recordings, complete editions, festival concerts, broadcasts, and other activities are being planned and celebrated the world over. Certainly, we have no shortage of music to sample. Whether or not you find the possibility of more orchestral Beethoven to explore intriguing, the fact is that the works he did leave us have proven themselves endlessly fascinating and expressively rewarding to many generations of music lovers. That situation, at least, doesn't seem likely to change anytime soon.

Track Listing

To access these audio tracks, please visit https://textbooks.rowman.com/beethoven-orchestral/

1. **"Egmont" Overture**

Piano Concerto No. 3 in C Minor
2. Allegro con brio
3. Largo
4. Rondo: Allegro

Symphony No. 5 in C Minor
5. Allegro con brio
6. Andante con moto
7. Scherzo. Allegro
8. Allegro

Recordings are licensed under permission of Naxos of America, Inc.
℗ Naxos of America, Inc.

www.ingramcontent.com/pod-product-compliance
Lightning Source LLC
Chambersburg PA
CBHW070829300426
44111CB00014B/2497